NIAGARA

Daredevils, Danger and Extraordinary Stories

Maria Da Silva and Andrew Hind

FOLK
LORE
PUBLISHING

The Publisher: Folklore Publishing
Website: www.folklorepublishing.com

Library and Archives Canada Cataloguing in Publication

Da Silva, Maria
    Niagara : daredevils, danger and extraordinary stories / by Maria Da Silva & Andrew Hind.

Includes bibliographical references.

ISBN 978-1-894864-86-2

    1. Daredevils—Niagara Falls (N.Y. and Ont.). 2. Niagara Falls (N.Y. and Ont.)—Miscellanea. 3. Niagara Falls Region (Ont.)—Miscellanea. I. Hind, Andrew II. Title.

FC3095.N5D37 2009   971.3'38   C2009-900199-3

Project Director: Faye Boer
Proofreader: Tracey Comeau
Project Editor: Kathy van Denderen
Cover Image: Courtesy of (left to right): 1. Falls shot, Photos.com; 2. Photos.com; 3. Murray Mold and the Daredevils Hall of Fame, Niagara Falls ; 4. Library of Congress Rare Book and Special Collections Division, Washington.
Photo credits: Every effort has been made to accurately credit the sources of photographs. Any errors or omissions should be reported directly to the publisher for correction in future editions. Photographs courtesy of Jeff Collens (pp. 113, 109, 130); Maria Da Silva (pp. 87, 124); Fallsview Casino Resort (pp. 241, 251); Library of Congress Rare Book and Special Collections Division, Washington, DC (cover, p. 216); Maid of the Mist Steamship Company (p. 153); Murray Mold and the Daredevil Hall of Fame, Niagara Falls (cover, pp. 42, 52, 66, 68); Niagara Falls Public Library (p. 91); Niagara Parks Commission (p. 157); the collection of the Rochester City Hall Photo Lab (p. 33); the collection of the Rochester Public Library Local History Division (p. 30).

We acknowledge the support of the Alberta Foundation for the Arts for our publishing program.

We acknowledge the financial support of the Government of Canada through the Book Publishing Industry Development Program (BPIDP) for our publishing activities.

 Canadian Patrimoine
Heritage canadien

PC:1

Contents

Dedication

THIS BOOK IS DEDICATED to all those countless individuals from Niagara's past whose bravery, imagination, enterprise and ambition have made this community so rich in fascinating stories.

Acknowledgments

WE WISH TO THANK those who were crucial in the completion of this book. Elaine Bald, former director of the IMAX Theatre, has our warmest appreciation for the way she embraced both us and our project. Her assistance in bringing the stories of the Niagara thrill-seekers to life was immeasurable. The current IMAX staff, including Murray Mold and Gil Perez, has been equally supportive and provided several of the daredevil images that help bring this book to life. Local historian and author George Bailey offered additional insight into the phenomenon that is daredevilry. Thanks must also go out to Jeff Collens, who generously provided copies of his vintage postcards for use in illustrating this book.

Other photos came from such diverse sources as the Maid of the Mist Steamship Company, the Rochester Public Library, the Niagara Parks Commission and the Niagara Falls Public Library. We wish to thank each of them for their assistance.

Special thanks to the staff at Fallsview Casino Resort for showing an interest in the book and providing us with unmatched hospitality. Without their support, our research trips to Niagara would have been more difficult and far less comfortable. A special thanks goes out to Kevin Harding, Communications Manager at the resort, who took time out of his schedule to lend his assistance.

Thank you to our publisher, Faye Boer, for her tireless support and for giving us the opportunity to write about one of our favorite places in Ontario. We hope the finished product justifies her faith in us.

Finally, we would be remiss if we didn't thank all those people—writers, members of historical societies, staff at area attractions—whose efforts to preserve and pass on the many fascinating stories related to Niagara Falls often goes unnoticed. These individuals have made our work a whole lot easier.

~❈~

Falling in love with the Niagara Region at an early age was easy for me. The magnificent attractions, the colorful gardens and of course the amazing Falls itself—there is so much to enjoy. But never did I dream that one day my passion for Niagara Falls would take the form of a book. I want to thank Andrew for opening a door in my life that I could never have imagined and taking me on as a co-writer. It seems the more we write, the more we learn about the places we visit; it's an endlessly exciting experience.

I'd also like to thank all the other people in my life for being so easygoing about the many trips undertaken in the name of research. But most of all, thank you to all those who made this book possible.

–Maria Da Silva

Maria has been my friend, cheerleader and greatest critic, and I thank her for being all those things. Her patience and advice often helped me while writing this book, as it does in my life in general. Maria's love of Niagara Falls was the inspiration for this book, and together we shared good times uncovering the many fascinating stories surrounding this natural wonder. Now, I believe my passion for Niagara matches her own.

I'd also like to thank everyone—and there were many—who made researching and writing this book easier. Their names don't appear on the cover, but each in their own way made important contributions, and I appreciate it.

–Andrew Hind

Introduction

MANY OF CANADA'S MOST unforgettable stories took place in Niagara Falls, a community with a history rich with colorful characters and headline-grabbing events. You'll find plenty of both in *Niagara: Daredevils, Danger and Extraordinary Stories.*

Meet brave (or reckless, depending on your point of view) daredevils who challenged the might of Niagara, diving into her waters, walking across the gorge on high wires and risking their lives in barrels. Experience the thrill of heroic rescues and the tragedy of terrible misfortunes. Delve into the origins of the booming tourism industry, the shadowy mysteries of the region and the lives of the scoundrels who preyed upon the innocent. And finally, watch as royalty, both the blue-blooded and the Hollywood variety, come to Niagara. There's something for everyone and a bit of everything.

While researching this book, we combed Niagara's long history for noteworthy tales. We found far too many than could comfortably fit within the confines of a single book so were forced to narrow it down significantly (a painful chore that meant cutting some very good yarns). Eventually, we settled on the most interesting stories and captured them in a series of vignettes.

Preserving history, whether in the form of physical objects or locales or merely on the written page, is important. History is fleeting. Memories fade and stories are quickly forgotten. We hope this book can play a role in keeping local history alive. Of course, the term "local history" is something of a misnomer in this particular case; though we do focus on a specific locality, Niagara Falls is a treasure enjoyed the world over, and therefore the stories are of universal interest and appeal.

We freely admit that this book is not a comprehensive look at Niagara Falls' history. That wasn't our intent, nor was it within the scope of this project. Instead, our goal was to entertain readers with a series of relatively short, lively tales written in such a fashion that, we hope, readers can't bear to put the book down. The reason for writing the book in this style was simple: we believe the best way to foster a genuine respect and passion for history is to make it both interesting and accessible to readers. A series of facts, told in a dry, scholarly fashion, just won't do that for the majority of us.

That said, a great deal of research (countless hours, in fact) went into this book, and historical accuracy was of utmost importance, but we hope it takes on a supporting role in these dramas. Center stage is reserved for the people and events themselves.

When one thinks of Niagara Falls, the thundering waters come to mind first, followed by the kitsch of Clifton Hill's wax museums and other attractions. The area's rich history, dating back more than two centuries, is largely unknown to the millions who visit every year. If we can give even some of these visitors a new appreciation for the people and events that helped shape the place they so enjoy, we consider our efforts well spent. Similarly, if our book encourages some people who may scorn Niagara Falls for its carnival-like atmosphere to visit this surprisingly diverse community, then we're happy.

But most of all, if we can entertain readers while sharing our passion for history, then we consider ourselves most fortunate. So find a comfortable chair, devote a few hours, and go back in time to experience some of Niagara's unforgettable events for yourself. We think you'll enjoy the journey.

CHAPTER ONE

A Brief History of Niagara Falls

THOUGH IT HAS A reputation that rests almost solely on the falls themselves and the kitschy entertainment of Clifton Hill, Niagara Falls is in fact one of the most historic communities in Ontario. When most of the province was still covered in dense wilderness in the early 1800s, farms and other industries were already thriving there, along with a robust tourist trade that drew thousands of American travelers every year.

This book presents several exciting stories from Niagara Falls' rich past spanning more than two centuries; to provide context and a foundation upon which these stories can rest, we've included a condensed history of the community and its region.

Characteristics and Formation

The waterfall we call Niagara Falls actually consists of three drops: Horseshoe Falls, American Falls and Bridal Veil Falls. Horseshoe Falls, the majority of which lies on the Canadian side of the border, and American Falls, located on the American side, are separated from one another by Goat

Island. The much smaller and less impressive Bridal Veil Falls is also on the American side, separated from the main falls by Luna Island. Although not exceptionally high, Niagara Falls is very wide and is particularly impressive in terms of the volume of water that passes over it (six million cubic feet every minute in high flow, or four million cubic feet on average). It is the most powerful waterfall in all of North America.

Niagara Falls was the child of a massive ice sheet, as much as two miles thick, that covered North America as far south as Kansas 12,000 years ago, during what is known as the Wisconsin glaciation (the last ice age). The Great Lakes were formed at the same time and by the same powerful forces.

The glacier receded and advanced several times during this era, acting as a giant bulldozer by scouring the landscape, shaping highlands here and cutting gorges there. This glacier quite literally crafted the landscape of today. When the ice eventually melted at the end of the ice age, the meltwaters formed the Great Lakes. Water from these newly formed lakes carved a path through the Niagara Escarpment en route to the Atlantic Ocean and created the Niagara River and gorge.

Constant erosion has seen the falls move over the passage of thousands of years. The original Niagara Falls—there was only one at the time, not the current three—was near the present site of Queenston, where it poured into a much larger

Lake Ontario. A constant eating away of the rock by the raging waters has seen the waterfall retreat almost seven miles southward at a rate of between one and seven feet per year, depending on the amount of water coming down from Lake Erie. At times in the distant past, for example, Lake Erie was cut off from the upper Great Lakes and therefore did not receive any of their water. This meant, naturally, less water flowing down the Niagara River and less erosive power. During such periods, the southward movement of Niagara Falls slowed considerably.

Niagara Falls separated into three distinct cataracts between 700 and 500 years ago, when the river encountered an obstacle, Goat Island, that caused it to split into two channels. On the eastern side of the island, the American Falls and Bridal Veil Falls took shape, and on the western side, the Horseshoe Falls.

Because the waters surrounding Goat Island are relatively shallow and studded with islets, erosion in this area is much slower than it is closer to the Canadian shore. Similarly, because only a relatively small amount of Niagara's flow plunges over the American Falls, it erodes much slower than the Horseshoe Falls.

In addition to receding almost seven miles, the Horseshoe Falls has also changed its shape over the centuries as a result of the erosion process. At first it was a shallow arch, by the 19th century it had became a distinctive horseshoe shape and today it is a gigantic inverted "V." Even though humans have diverted more than half of the Niagara River's water for hydroelectrical purposes, the current of the river as it flows over the falls remains strong enough that erosion continues to shape them.

The Horseshoe Falls retreats about one foot every 10 years, slowing eating away more and more of the river bed to create an ever-expanding gorge. The American and Bridal Veil falls, on the other hand, receive too little water to scour out a gorge of their own. Instead, they will eventually become a steep rapid until Horseshoe Falls passes Goat Island, at which time all of the river's water will be sent over Horseshoe Falls and they will dry up. The timeframe for this to occur is said to be a couple thousand years from now; the falls as we know them will remain for a long, long time.

Early Years

The first Europeans to see Niagara arrived in the mid-1600s. They were French explorers and missionaries, driven by a desire to expand the fur trade and convert Natives to their religion. No one knows for sure who was the first European to see the mighty falls—perhaps it was Samuel de Champlain or Sieur Robert de la Salle—but we do know who was the first to record his impressions: French missionary Father Louis Hennepin, who was awestruck by the sight in 1678. His account of the falls was a dramatic misrepresentation, depicting them as being much higher than they really are and including a non-existent range of mountains in the background. Hennepin's account, misleading though it was, formed the basis for our understanding of the falls for more than a century.

The name "Niagara" emerged around this time, though its roots are somewhat murky, and theories differ as to the origin of the name. Some suggest "Niagara" is derived from the name of a tribe of the Neutral Confederacy that resided in the region. Others say it derives from the name Onguiaahra, which appears on maps as early as 1641, and was the result of attempts by Jesuit missionaries to establish a written equivalent for the Iroquoian name for the area. The generally accepted meaning of the word is either "the neck," referring to the Niagara River, or "thundering waters," in respect to the falls themselves.

In any event, more than half a century passed before Hennepin wrote his fantasized account of the first permanent European inhabitation of Niagara. In 1721, the French established a trading post at Lewiston and a few years later built a sturdy stone fortress, Fort Niagara, at the point where the Niagara River flows into Lake Ontario. From this point on, the Niagara region became the focus of an imperial tug-of-war between France and Britain, with the victory prize being domination over all of North America. The contest was settled once and for all by the Seven Years' War, which ended in 1763 and saw France cede all of her territories in Canada to Great Britain. A year later, in 1764, the British built Fort Erie at the mouth of the Niagara River and Lake Erie to cement control over the strategic region.

Most of the early settlers in what is now Niagara Falls were United Empire Loyalists. Arriving after the end of the American Revolution (1775–83), they were Americans who had remained steadfastly loyal to King and Country and as a result were persecuted and ostracized after the British defeat. Thousands sought new homes in Canada, where they were forced to start anew. Many settled along the Niagara River.

Other early settlers were African Americans, predominantly slaves escaping from the American South. Upper Canada (what is now Ontario) became the first place in the British Empire to abolish slavery, when Governor General John Graves Simcoe introduced legislation to that effect in 1793 from the provincial capital of Newark (Niagara-on-the-Lake). As a result, the area became a haven for slaves seeking to throw off the shackles of servitude and a principle terminal for the Underground Railway. Many of the escaped slaves chose to establish permanent roots in Niagara Falls.

The War of 1812 saw the entire Niagara Region erupt in a storm of violence, bloodshed and misery, as the United States sought to absorb Canada into the young republic. Although battles took place all over North America, the bloodiest and most decisive (including the Battle of Lundy's Lane and the Battle of Queenston Heights) were fought along the Niagara frontier. The eventual outcome was a stalemate, and the Treaty of Ghent reestablished the Niagara River as the border between the two nations. But the manner in which the War of 1812 shaped Niagara can be seen in the historic forts, monuments, museums, cemeteries and memorials found throughout the region.

Birth of Tourism and Birth of a Town

Although the War of 1812 was not quickly forgotten, people on both sides of the border were willing to let bygones be bygones. Evidence of this can be seen in the birth of the tourism industry that began almost as soon as the conflict ended and saw thousands of wealthy Americans every year make a trip to the falls. Soon, hotels and showmen catering to these travelers appeared, and official guides began making a living taking sightseers on a tour of the area's major points of interest.

By the time the first *Maid of the Mist* steamboat was launched on the American side of the falls in 1846, as many as 50,000 summer visitors came to Niagara Falls every year. This number only rose when, a decade later, the world's first suspension bridge, which included a plank roadway for foot passengers and horse-drawn carriages on its underside, was completed, linking Niagara Falls, Canada, to Niagara Falls, New York. Niagara Falls became the best-known tourist destination in North America.

As the crowds grew, a rowdy strip of concession stands, hotels and carnival booths sprung up around the falls, all eager to grab a piece of the tourist dollar. As a result of this rapid and unplanned development, many people began to worry about the future of the falls. Would this wonder of nature, a rare treasure, be desecrated by humans? It was a real concern among the public. Accordingly, in 1878, Lord Dufferin, the governor general of Canada, proposed that a strategy be developed to preserve the natural beauty of Niagara Falls.

Seven years later, the Niagara Parks Commission was founded to preserve and enhance the natural splendor of the falls and the shores along the entire Niagara River shore. The showpiece of the Niagara Parks Commission, a 154-acre park adjacent to the Horseshoe Falls and named Queen Victoria Park after the reigning monarch, was opened in 1888. This extensive area of greenland ensured that visitors taking in the glorious, mist-shrouded spectacle of the falls would be surrounded not by hucksters and concession stands but by a more harmonious setting of trees and gardens.

As tourism was developing so, too, was the shape of the community that serviced the travelers and sightseers. The Town of Niagara Falls did not exist for much of the 19th century. It is actually a composite of a number of small villages in the area, each with a unique character that helped create the identity of the Niagara Falls we know today.

Chippawa was the first of these villages to emerge. It can trace its origins back to the construction of the Portage Road, which allowed traffic to bypass the rapids and falls of the Niagara River. Opened in 1790, its northern terminus was Queenston, the southern end at the mouth of the Chippawa Creek. It was here that Chippawa developed, dependent on the river traffic for much of its prosperity. Shortly thereafter, another community developed around the intersection of Portage Road (Main Street), Lundy's Lane and Ferry Street. Named Drummondville, it grew rapidly and was incorporated in 1831.

The construction of the bridge spanning the Niagara River, traversed by both train and horse-drawn traffic, was a boon to the region. It was also a magnet for businesses and others eager to capitalize on this traffic. Soon, the village of Elgin emerged around what is now the lower end of Bridge Street. It was a major divisional point on the Great Western Railway and so prospered. In 1856, Elgin merged with a small hamlet to the south that centered upon the Clifton Hill area. The enlarged town took the name Clifton.

In 1881, Clifton changed its name to the Town of Niagara Falls. Not to be outdone, the following year, Drummondville became the Village of Niagara Falls. In 1904, the two communities amalgamated to create the City of Niagara Falls. Within two years, three large hydroelectric generating plants began operating in the area around the Horseshoe Falls. Inexpensive and plentiful electricity, along with excellent rail transportation and close proximity to the U.S. market, soon attracted many manufacturing industries to Niagara Falls, thus ensuring the new city's growth and prosperity. Of course, the tourism industry remained vibrant as well.

In 1963, the adjacent Township of Stamford amalgamated with the city. Niagara Falls completed its geographic growth when, in 1970, Chippawa, Willoughby Township and a small portion of Crowland Township also became part of Niagara Falls.

Niagara Falls Today

Niagara Falls is a city of 82,000 residents, its population dwarfed by the masses of tourists (as many as 15 million) that visit every year. It's a community of contradictions. The majesty and grandeur of the falls, surrounded by beautifully groomed parks and pristine gardens, exist side by side with the noise and energy of the Clifton Hill district with its neon lights, fast-food outlets and carnival atmosphere. It's a place where top-of-the-line hotels, such as the Niagara Fallsview Casino Resort, operate alongside a string of cheap motels. And it's a location with a rich and varied history, full of dramatic stories and notable landmarks, where the focus tends to be more on the thrill of the moment than reflecting on the past.

The falls are the main attraction of the Niagara region, and the allure of Clifton Hill's varied attractions are hard to ignore. And that's how it should be. However, it's our hope—and certainly the goal of this book—that once people have had their fill of these sights, they might take an interest in the people, places and events that helped shape the community that countless millions enjoy today.

CHAPTER TWO

Daredevils—The Aerialists

MOST PEOPLE ARE CONTENT to simply view the stunning wonder that is Niagara Falls and its turbulent river. Others want more, to become a part of the spectacle, to pit themselves against the awesome power of the falls and the rapids. These brave—some would say, foolhardy—individuals are Niagara's daredevils, and for almost 200 years they have risked their lives in search of fame and fortune. Many perished in the attempt, and even those who survived found wealth and glory elusive.

The methods by which daredevils have challenged Niagara demonstrate the full inventiveness of humankind, but during the 19th century, the most common daredevils were individuals loosely defined as aerialists. Some, including Niagara's first daredevil, were divers who chose to leap from great heights into the waters of the abyss below. Although diving into the gorge took a great deal of courage and skill, the stunt itself took no more than a few seconds to complete, and onlookers, who were expected to make generous donations to the daredevil, were left wanting more. That said, jumpers continued to make a splash for more than a century. In 1908 alone, Bobby Leach, an English circus performer, made half a dozen jumps into the Niagara. The last man to dive into the river, Vincent Taylor, leaped from the Upper Steel Arch Bridge in 1927.

Diving into the river was a novelty the first few times, but it rapidly lost its appeal. The public wanted something more dramatic, something that would hold their attention for a much longer period. They wanted a show. Enter the tightrope walker. There was a real thrill in watching a man (or woman) cross from one side of the Niagara to the other on a narrow strand of rope suspended at a dizzying height above the river. Because most tightrope walkers had a circus background, they were first-class showmen who knew how to dress up the act with outlandish costumes, comedic performances and daring twists that held the audiences in rapt attention.

The Great Blondin was the first and arguably the most celebrated of the tightrope walkers, but many imitators followed. Between 1859 and 1897, a total of 11 different tightrope walkers crossed the Niagara gorge, several of them performing the feat multiple times. Perhaps because there were so many of them, these daredevils developed bitter rivalries with one another, going to great lengths (and sometimes stooping to surprising lows) to one-up their competitors. Certainly, the newspapers reported extensively on the animosity—it made for great print, after all—and this fed the public's interest.

By the 1890s, however, the fickle viewing audience was demanding greater thrills and more danger than tightrope walkers could provide. Their attention turned elsewhere, specifically to those willing to risk their lives by navigating the whirlpool and rapids, or better yet, by going over the falls themselves.

While the golden era of Niagara's tightrope walkers ended with the closing of the 19th century, a few individuals have since stepped forward to follow in Blondin's death-defying footsteps. In fact, the last to do so, Phillipe Petit, who in 1986 walked a 50-foot-long cable suspended 170 feet above the river, recreated Blondin's high-wire act for the IMAX movie *Niagara: Miracle, Myths and Magic.*

Sam Patch

Throughout the morning of Wednesday, October 7, 1829, rain had fallen steadily and caused a heavy mist that blurred Niagara Falls. But when the mist finally parted, the gathered crowd could scarcely believe what they were seeing. A young man wearing a black vest and white trousers stood atop a specially built platform on Goat Island, in the middle of the falls and some 85 feet above the Niagara River. He acknowledged his audience by bowing his head in a silent sign of welcome.

It was about 4:00 PM when 22-year-old Sam Patch moved forward to the edge of the platform, took a deep breath and jumped into the abyss below. He plunged down with the crashing water as a backdrop, his arms slightly in front of him and his feet apart, hitting the water feet first with a mighty splash. He sank into the water like a rock, and for a time a breathless silence hung over the crowd. Had the foolhardy young man died? Then, to everyone's relief, Sam's head bobbed to the surface, and he waved to the crowd. The crowd roared with approval. In that moment, a Niagara legend was born.

Sam Patch came into the world in 1807 in Pawtucket, Rhode Island, where, as soon as he was old enough, he began working as a child laborer spinning cotton in a mill. When he wasn't working, Patch and other boyhood friends entertained themselves and the young ladies by jumping off the mill dam at Pawtucket Falls, a height of 50 feet. Going one step beyond his peers, young Patch would climb atop the mill and leap into the water from that commanding position, a jump of 80 feet. You could say that even at an early age, Sam had the devil in him—"a daredevil," that is.

By the time he was in his early 20s, Sam was working at a mill in Paterson, New Jersey, and was jumping off even higher spots. What's more, he began to attract crowds as his feats spread through word of mouth and were advertised in local newspapers. His first staged stunt occurred on September 30, 1827. A large crowd gathered to witness the daredevil jump off the 70-foot-high Passaic Falls in New Jersey. It's been suggested that Sam's first plunge was made "with the view of getting rid of the cares and troubles of life," having recently been rejected by a young woman he was trying to court.

Attempted suicide or not, the jump was a success and brought adulation his way, along with a small purse of money. Sam repeated this jump at least two more times, and on yet another occasion he jumped from a height of 100 feet at Hoboken, New Jersey, from atop a ship's mast. By this time, he was making headlines in the press as "Patch, the New Jersey Jumper."

Patch became addicted to the cheers and the adrenaline. He continued to leap—the higher the stunt the better—jumping from bridges, factory walls and even ships' masts. Over the next two years, he probably made dozens of jumps from varying heights, slowly adding to his reputation. But true fame, the kind that legends are born of, only came when he jumped from atop Niagara Falls. It made him a North American celebrity, and, as Niagara's first stunter, he set the bar by which all future Niagara daredevils measured themselves.

The thrilling spectacle was the idea of a group of Niagara Falls businessmen who wanted a stunt that would draw tourists. They invited Patch to town in October 1829 to perform his act of derring-do as part of a larger show that included the demolition by dynamite of a huge rocky shelf in the Niagara gorge and a decorated sailing ship that would be sent down the river and over the falls. In the end, the show was a bust; the explosions were pitifully small and lost amid the roar of the falls, the ship ran aground on a rock midstream and Sam Patch arrived late so did not jump on the appointed date.

Eager to please the crowds, Patch scheduled a jump for October 7. It had been raining, and there was a heavy mist that morning, but by three o'clock in the afternoon, visibility improved enough to allow the show to go on. At 4:00 PM, Sam appeared on a platform extending out into the gorge from Goat Island, wearing a black vest and white trousers. He acknowledged his audience, moved forward, took a deep breath and jumped feet first.

William Lyon Mackenzie, a well-known figure who owned the Toronto *Colonial Advocate* newspaper, was present during the stunt and later wrote:

The celebrated Sam Patch leaped over the Falls of Niagara into the vast abyss below…While the boats below were on the lookout for him he had in one minute reached the shore unnoticed and unhurt, and was heard on the beach singing as merrily as if altogether unconscious of having performed an act

*so extraordinary as almost to appear an incredible
fable. Sam Patch has immortalized himself.*

Sam, however, was not content. Bad weather
and the delay of his arrival drew a disappointingly
small crowd for this jump, and relatively little
profit, so he announced that a repeat of the jump
would take place a few days later, on October 17.
To generate excitement, he announced that this
new jump would be performed from an even
greater height—a raised platform built atop Goat
Island. Inserting an advertisement in the *Colonial
Advocate*, he explained:

*Having been thus disappointed, the owners of Goat
Island have generously granted me the use of it for
nothing so that I may have a chance from an equally
generous public, to obtain some remuneration for
my long journey hither, as well as affording me an
opportunity for supporting the reputation I have
gained by aeronautical feats never before attempted
either in the Old or New World.*

Saturday, October 17, was another cloudy and
rainy day, but Sam refused to disappoint the crowds.
Three hundred people had paid a toll to watch from
Goat Island, and hundreds more lined the river
shores. When he emerged, he wore a sailor's jacket
and a scarf at his neck, one of the showman-style
costumes that would become his trademark. He
climbed the ladder and stood atop the platform for
almost 10 minutes, swaying dangerously in the

wind. He barely moved during this time, his eyes focused on the gorge below as if contemplating the 130-foot drop, 40 feet more than he had ever attempted before.

Then, at exactly 3:00 PM, he bowed to the crowds on both sides of the river and kissed the corners of an American flag. The crowd erupted in a roar of approval. The applause had barely died down when Patch leapt. He once again defied all odds and miraculously survived, swimming to the American shore amid cheers and a little storm of white handkerchiefs.

Patch was hailed for his bravado and ability and was treated like a hero; wherever he went, people bought him drinks, star-struck fans couldn't wait to meet him and women blushed in the presence of his youthful good looks. Niagara Falls adored Sam Patch, and he in turn loved the attention.

For whatever reason, he then decided to move his act to Genesee Falls, near Rochester, New York, where he would tackle the 99-foot-high falls. On Friday, November 6, 1829, in front of an estimated 7000 to 8000 spectators (which almost equaled the population of Rochester at the time), Sam Patch went out onto a rock ledge and took his place above the middle of the falls. But he added a new twist to his performance. Before leaping, he stunned the crowd by throwing a pet bear cub over the edge and into the water far below. Miraculously, the cub bobbed to the surface, and thousands of relived onlookers applauded as the bear frantically swam for shore.

Now it was Sam's turn to take center stage. He bowed to the crowd and happily waved to them. Cheers arose from the crowd, and it was obvious to everyone that he relished the adoration. Then the crowd grew silent, so that the only sound was the roar of the falls. Shortly after 3:00 PM, he took his leap. Less than a minute later, it was all over. Sam Patch had successfully conquered another waterfall, to the amazement and approval of thousands.

But Sam wasn't content. He was disappointed with the size of the crowd and the amount of money raised, so he decided to repeat the stunt, this time increasing the height of the jump to 125 feet by constructing a 25-foot stand atop the falls. The date was set for one week later, on Friday, November 13, 1829. Sam selected Friday the 13th on purpose, because the day was considered to be lethally unlucky and would undoubtedly make for a larger crowd. He also built excitement by promising that this would be "Sam's last jump." It turned out to be just that.

On the afternoon of the 13th, as many as 12,000 people gathered along the sides of the gorge to watch his latest feat of daring. Anticipation crackled through the air, and when Sam finally appeared, a great cheer erupted from the masses. People pressed closer to watch the unfolding spectacle.

Like all of Niagara's most memorable daredevils, Sam Patch, the Jersey Jumper, was a master of shameless self-promotion. This flyer ominously advertised his last jump; Patch couldn't have known at the time how literal the words would become.

~~✺~~

People reported seeing Sam sway as he stood on the diving platform and noted that his eyes looked blank. Some were convinced that he was "considerably intoxicated" and "quite tipsy," although those closest to him were adamant that he was sober. After a short and largely incoherent speech, Sam Patch leapt into the chasm. But even here accounts vary. Many of the witnesses disagreed on whether he actually jumped or perhaps accidentally fell.

At first, his leap began as gracefully as his previous ones, but one-third of the way down, things went terribly wrong. His body veered sideways, and the crowd watched in horror as he fell with his arms flailing wildly in the air. It proved impossible to right himself, so that instead of achieving his normal feet-first vertical entry into the water, he hit lengthwise and with a grisly-sounding impact that was clearly heard, even by spectators atop the gorge.

To everyone's dismay, Sam didn't surface. As the minutes passed with still no sign of him, the excitement that had brought spectators to the falls turned into horror. A deathly silence hung over the crowd; no one could bring themselves to speak. Finally accepting the truth, they turned and walked away. The haunted spectators would play the awful scene over and over again in their dreams.

Rumors soon spread that Sam Patch had finally had enough of being a daredevil and decided to stage his death to leave behind an immortal legend. Many believed that "the New Jersey Jumper" had survived the fall and swam to a cave at the base of the falls, where he had hidden dry clothes and a bottle of rum, to wait until nightfall before slipping away.

In the days and weeks to come, people swore they saw him in places such as New York and Boston, and newspapers printed letters supposedly written in his hand. Some even suggested that the Sam Patch who made the jump was a straw man weighed down to ensure he sank and that the real Patch stood among the crowd to watch he hoax unfold.

But, just as with any rumor, the truth usually surfaces, and so too did Sam Patch's body. It was early spring 1840, and a man named Silas Hudson was walking along the lower reaches of Genesee River when he spotted what he thought was garbage floating just below the ice. Hudson kicked through the ice, and up popped the frozen body of the ill-fated leaper. Most of his hair was gone, the face was battered and distorted, and a deep gash was over one eye, but the signature clothing made identification of the corpse easy. There was now no denying the horrible truth: Sam Patch, Niagara's first stunter, had made one too many jumps.

Even before Sam was buried in the little Charlotte cemetery near the mouth of the Genesee, local ministers and newspapers blamed the public for his death. They suggested that the crowd present at his last stunt had urged him to jump, goading him into making a suicidal leap, and put the guilt of Sam's death clearly on them. The reality was, however, that Sam Patch had become addicted to the applause and adulation. He needed no encouragement to jump.

Sam Patch was a folk hero in America, a living legend in life and in death. In fact, like an early version of Elvis, many refused to believe he had actually died, and he remained popular for decades. Patch was even the star of children's books nearly half a century after his passing.

～◦✕◦～

Sam Patch was a modern celebrity, a man born into obscurity who had made a name for himself, a legend if you will, simply by leaping off waterfalls.

He became so famous in his short time as a jumper that, like modern icons who perish before their time, many believed he was not dead. But a simple headstone in a small cemetery near Charlotte, New York, proves such beliefs to be little more than wishful thinking or fantastic tales. There, largely forgotten today, lies Sam Patch—the New Jersey Jumper, the first Niagara Daredevil, and an icon of his era.

Maria Spelterini

The young woman is a stunning beauty, her exotic looks leaving men struggling for air and women jealous at the attention she receives. On this particular day, however, all who look on her are breathless.

As usual, her attire makes a statement. She is dressed in an unusual, tight-fitting costume with pale green boots and a hat that sits delicately upon her glossy, raven-black hair. The woman looks out at the gathered crowd with eyes that sparkle with the flame of youth, smiling confidently. Slowly, the daylight disappears from her eyes, as a blindfold is secured at the back of her head. She takes a deep breath, concentrating, eliminating all distractions. She focuses on her body and its every movement.

Slowly, gently, she places one foot forward and feels for the familiar rope. Molding her foot over the cord, she allows it to absorb her weight. Then another step is taken. And another. She hears the roar of the rapidly flowing water far below, calling out to her, urging her to plummet into its grasp. But this day—July 8, 1876—the mighty waters of Niagara would not claim her, for she has performed this stunt many times, and she walks the tightrope with fearless, familiar ease.

The Niagara River didn't swallow up Maria Spelterini that day more than 130 years ago, but time has. For a brief period she was the darling of the newspapers, a woman who was written about with enthusiasm and admiration. The public loved her, to the extent that her fame matched that of any Niagara daredevil who had come before her.

But Maria Spelterini was, and remains today, an enigma.

Incredibly, despite the acclaim she achieved in her day, not much is really known about the first and only woman to cross the Niagara River on a tightrope. Maria Spelterini hailed from Livorno, Italy, where she was born around 1853, and made her first appearance with her father's circus troupe when only three years old. A lifetime spent walking across slender threads made her as comfortable walking a high-wire as most people are walking the street.

Sometime later, she established a solo career and achieved great renown as a tightrope walker in a number of European cities. A highly publicized tour during 1872–73 saw her perform in Moscow, St. Petersburg, on the Isle of Jersey and in France.

Eventually, Maria took her act to the United States, lured there by the celebrations commemorating America's centennial. Exhibitions and festivities were planned in every community across the country, but none topped the plan for Niagara Falls. It was here that Maria Spelterini's name was written into the history books and where she etched herself in popular imagination by becoming Niagara's first female daredevil.

Maria was no ordinary woman. She was different from the conservative Victorian females of that time, outgoing and confident when such traits were frowned upon in the "fairer sex." The idea of a woman tempting fate by performing dangerous stunts was unseemly and unladylike. After all, this was an era when women were expected to stay home and maintain a certain decorum, leaving the spotlight for the men. But not Maria. She had fire in her soul and would not be bound into slavery by the conventions of the day. She craved freedom, and she found it while walking the tightrope. When she was up there, high above the ground, it felt to her like walking on a cloud—and she did not allow anyone to clip her wings.

Always ambitious, ever the entertainer, Maria was constantly searching for new challenges. By 1876, she had set her sights on walking a tightrope across the Niagara. Perhaps she was inspired by the exploits and subsequent fame of those who had already performed the feat. The first tightrope walker at Niagara was Jean Francois Gravelet, better known as the Great Blondin, who crossed the river almost 20 times in 1859 and 1860. A few other brave and talented individuals followed in his footsteps, but none made the splash that Maria Spelterini did.

Spelterini made her Niagara debut on July 8, 1876. She had actually been scheduled to appear on July 4 but bad weather forced her to postpone the event for four days. When she finally made her appearance, all agreed that the young woman was well worth the wait. She was a shapely, buxom 23-year-old whose physical charms drew almost as much attention as her aerial performance. Several newspaper reporters wrote glowingly of the "superbly built female funambulist [tightrope walker] in flesh-colored tights, a tunic of scarlet, a sea-green bodice and ñeat green buskins." Maria Spelterini was born to be a star.

And she had the talent to back up her beauty. As Maria stepped out onto the tightrope spanning the Niagara River, the hot summer sun beamed down on her like a spotlight. She seemed completely unfazed by the oppressive heat, unlike the spectators, who desperately tried to keep cool by hiding under umbrellas and fanning themselves. For this, her first performance, Maria, traveling on a two-inch-thick wire that one newspaper described as a "gossamer web," stepped gracefully and confidently from the American side to the Canadian side.

For the trip back, she walked in time to waltz music provided by brass bands stationed on either shore, dancing effortlessly to the regal tunes. It was a breathtaking performance. She made crossing Niagara look as easy as a walk in the park; for her, it probably was. But Maria was not about to stop with one performance. More importantly, she was smart enough to know that audiences would quickly grow bored with a simple repeat of her first performance. She threw a dramatic new wrinkle into each of her subsequent performances.

"The Signorina," as she was known to her adoring public, went on to perform four more of her daring acts over the next few weeks. On July 12, in place of boots, she wore peach baskets on her feet, walking forwards and backwards on the rope. People's memories returned to the feats of the Great Blondin, who performed at the exact same location just below the Whirlpool Rapids Bridge 16 years earlier. If anything, however, Maria made crossing the 800-foot gorge look easier than did her illustrious predecessor. "Walking across the river does not display the artist's nerves half as much as the different performances I propose to give on the rope," she was quoted as saying.

To demonstrate her skill and daring, Maria crossed the gorge blindfolded and backwards on July 19, and even with her hands and feet shackled on July 22. Each time, the act seemed completely effortless. For her final performance of July 27, she chose to walk the tightrope once more with the peach baskets on her feet.

Then, as quickly as she appeared, Maria Spelterini vanished. Nothing was ever heard from her again. For a woman who craved the headlines, and whose stunning feats and equally stunning looks commanded attention wherever she went, to simply disappear without a trace is mysterious. But disappear she did, so completely that it was as if she had been swallowed up by the mists that rose from the falls.

Though several attempts have been made over the years to trace her later career and to fill in the gaps of her life, these have all been in vain. The fact is, no one really knows what became of her. Her performance of July 27, 1876, was the last time she appears in history.

Some people have suggested that Maria Spelterini retired from show business after the Centennial celebrations concluded, therefore sliding off the pages of newspapers. It's certainly possible that, having conquered Niagara so effortlessly, she was left without any challenges worthy of her daring and decided to go out while on top. But could she so easily give up the limelight she adored?

Others have suggested that she married shortly thereafter and only disappeared, figuratively speaking, by taking another name. And then there is a final possibility: that "Maria Spelterini" was nothing more than a stage name, a guise that could be easily slipped into and out of as necessary. Most of the great showmen of the day, whether they were tightrope walkers or entertainers of another stripe, used exotic stage names to set themselves apart. So, there is always the possibility that the persona of Maria Spelterini was simply cast aside by the woman behind the name.

The truth? No one knows for certain; maybe no one ever will.

What is certain is that her disappearance only enhances our fascination. Maria Spelterini is one of Niagara's most compelling mysteries, one that in all likelihood will forever intrigue the human mind. She left us with more questions than answers, including the most important: who was she?

Stephen Peer

Some people will do just about anything to gain a little fame. For many men and even some women in the 19th century, Niagara Falls represented an opportunity to write oneself into the history books. The heart-pumping thrill of challenging the wild waters of Niagara, either by racing through the rapids in a barrel or crossing the gorge on tight-ropes strung high above the white-capped waters, captured immediate attention for any individual willing to put his—or her—life on the line. If you succeeded in your reckless act of bravery, it meant world fame.

Most of the daredevils who gravitated toward Niagara Falls were foreigners, but a few locals stepped forward to challenge the mighty falls. The earliest was tightrope walker Stephen Peer, whose breathtaking high-wire antics made him a local legend. Unfortunately, he's best remembered today not for his bravery and skill but for the untimely and mysterious nature of his demise.

The last half of the 19th century was the golden era for the tightrope walkers, also known as funambulists, and many were drawn to Niagara Falls. They tested their courage and ability over the dizzying heights of the Niagara River gorge, wowing audiences with performances set against the spectacular backdrop of the falls themselves. One of these famously acrobatic men was Jean Francois Gravelet, better known as the Great Blondin, achieved lasting fame with his exploits in 1859 and 1860 when he became the first person to walk a tightrope across the gorge.

Later, others began to follow Blondin, hoping to achieve a similar level of celebrity. Among them was Henry Bellini, who came to Niagara in 1873 and stretched his rope across the gorge just north of the American Falls. Bellini gave a number of performances over a period of several weeks and was widely acclaimed for his showmanship. While in Niagara, Henry Bellini hired an assistant named Stephen Peer to help set up his acts.

During the 19th century, the tightrope walkers were the most flamboyant and popular of Niagara's daredevils.

~⁘~

Peer, who was born in Stamford Township (now part of Niagara Falls) in 1840, was no stranger to ropewalking. He had been an impressionable 19-year-old when he saw Blondin perform at Niagara, and the great ropewalker soon became his hero. From that time on, Peer was determined to become a tightrope walker himself and establish fame, just as his hero before him had done, by someday giving a show at Niagara. Over the following years, Peer began to develop his body, molding it into the perfect balance of strength and agility. He exercised his mind as well, until he had established a mastery of concentration.

Though Peer worked as a painter by trade, he spent every spare moment perfecting his skills as a ropewalker. At first, he crafted makeshift ropes by twisting grapevines together, strung them between trees in the family orchard and practiced walking from trunk to trunk at a safe height. Soon his confidence increased, and he began to give performances publicly along Main Street, his rope strung between the second floors of two hotels on opposite sides of the street.

Then, in 1873, came the opportunity to work with the great Henry Bellini. Peer was initially thrilled to be in the presence of the talented tightrope walker, but the thrill began to fade when he realized that his role as an assistant consisted solely of helping set up and care for the ropes. Not much fun. Worse, it was a tease. He was close to his dream of walking across the Niagara gorge, so close he could literally reach out and touch it, but he had to remain in the shadows as another man received the accolades he so badly desired.

Soon Peer could not resist the temptation to cross the ropes himself, and he approached his boss about taking a more active role in the act. Bellini refused, not wanting to share the spotlight with anyone.

But this did not stop Peer. He waited patiently for an opportunity when Bellini was absent between shows then made his move. When the occasion finally presented itself, Peer showed no hesitation. He reached for the balancing pole, took a deep breath to calm his emotions, and started out on the rope from the Canadian side at "a positive trot," as the *Niagara Falls, New York, Gazette* reported. At about the midway point of the crossing, Peer stopped and went through some of Blondin's most difficult acrobatic and gymnastic feats, astonishing the viewers on shore with the ease, grace and skill with which he performed.

While the performance was in progress and the crowds in awe, Bellini returned. His face twisted in rage when he saw another man, his assistant, no less, walking on the very ropes by which he made his fame. When the crowd cheered Peer's latest routine, something in Bellini's mind snapped. This country bumpkin, this nobody, was making a mockery of him and his talent. He wouldn't stand for it. No man made a fool of the Great Bellini.

The maddened showman pushed his way through the crowd and began to cut through the rope with a knife. As soon as onlookers realized what he was doing, they frantically tried to restrain him. It took several men, but Bellini was pulled to the ground before the rope could be severed, and Peer completed his crossing without incident.

Because Stephen Peer was a hometown boy, the crowd was understandably enraged at Bellini for his reckless actions endangering Peer's life. They made it clear he was no longer welcome and chased him out of town.

Amazingly enough, despite his obvious talent and the warmth in which he was received by his hometown crowd, Peer waited 14 years for the opportunity to present his own show across the Niagara Gorge.

He might have been sparked by the 1886 return of the Great Bellini, who got widespread coverage in local papers for his dive from the Upper Suspension Bridge. Never mind that he broke three ribs and was knocked unconscious by the impact, the stunt made him the talk of the town once again. Perhaps Peer felt the need to upstage his former boss, the man who had tried to kill him rather than share the spotlight.

On June 22, 1887, the 47-year-old "local Blondin," as he was known in the papers, did just that with a performance that wrote him into the Niagara history books. It was unusually windy that afternoon, but Peer was determined to try something never before accomplished: a dangerous crossing of the gorge using a slender wire cable only five-eights of an inch thick, instead of a rope. In light of the buffeting winds and thin cable, many felt the stunt was reckless at best, if not actually suicidal.

Peer did not think of rescheduling or using a thicker rope, and, at 4:00 PM, he stepped forward from the crowd, wearing pink tights and carrying a 45-pound balancing pole. For a time, he simply stood there, looking at the cable that was stretched across the gorge between the Cantilever and Suspension bridges (now the Whirlpool Bridge and the Pen Central Bridge). Some thought he was weighing his options, considering whether to go forward or back out, when in reality he was simply focusing on the task ahead.

Then, placing one foot in front of the other, moving at a steady pace, he made his way out onto the wire. The wind was a hindrance that threatened to upset his balance, and the cable, which was not properly secured, swayed and bowed under his weight. At times, he lost his balance and almost fell into the yawning chasm below, but with the encouragement of thousands of spectators on both banks of the river, his walk was a complete success.

When he finally reached the American side, Peer was completely exhausted and returned to the Canadian side in a carriage along the Suspension Bridge, where he was welcomed by applauding spectators. Stephen Peer had become the first (and as it turned out, only) Niagara native to walk a tightrope across the Niagara River.

Though he received great praise for his death-defying act, Peer made little financial gain. A hat was passed around the crowd, and when it was returned to Peer, to his disappointment, he found that only $35 had been collected. The press called it "a mean and paltry return for the only man who ever walked such a slender rope across the chasm of the Niagara River." Although the money was not what he had expected, Peer was satisfied with his own accomplishment and looked forward to many more in the future.

Unfortunately, his future was tragically cut short. Three days after his successful stunt, while he was still the toast of the town, Niagara Falls found itself in a state of shock when the headline of the *Hamilton Daily Spectator* read, "Peer the Rope-walker, Suicide."

But had Stephen Peer really committed suicide? The facts surrounding his death were, and remain, in dispute.

Since his act on June 22, Peer had taken to drinking at the nearby Elgin House Hotel, celebrating his success with round after round of whiskey and beer. On the day of his death, he was seen drinking heavily in the hotel, with a local man and a stranger. After hours of throwing back drinks, the three men were spotted together near Peer's wire. That was the last time the daredevil was seen alive.

By 8:30 that night, Peer was missed by friends and family. No one had seen him for hours, and people began to worry. A search team was formed, and with information his brother received from William Leery, the owner of Elgin House Hotel, they focused their attention near the ropes where Stephen Peer had become famous only days before. With lantern in hand, Peer's worry-sick brother was lowered over the edge of the gorge and down to the river bank 45 feet below. There, at the bottom of the cliff, lay the lifeless body of Stephen Peer. His body was broken and twisted in an unnatural position, and his head had hit the rocks with such impact that the skull was split wide open. Death had to have come instantly.

Peer's lifeless body was gently raised to the top of the cliff by ropes. Later, it was taken to Elgin House, where it laid waiting for a coroner. The coroner's inquest labeled Peer's death a suicide, but many Niagara residents simply did not believe the verdict.

Why would Peer commit suicide at the peak of his career? He was basking in the glow of his accomplishments, and greater fame and perhaps fortune lay ahead for him. Suicide made no sense. Maybe his death was simply an accident. Perhaps he had tried to walk the tightrope after his night of drinking and, losing his footing, fell to his death in the abyss below. A story began circulating that his two companions on that fateful night dared Peer to cross the wire. Drunk and wearing hard-soled shoes, he didn't make it far before apparently falling to his doom.

And then darker theories emerged. Was Peer, in fact, murdered? Some suggested that he was pushed off the ledge by his companions or that he was murdered elsewhere and his body dumped into the gorge to mask the crime. Others even insinuated that Bellini, possibly still embarrassed by his less-than-glorious stunt a year earlier, might have returned to take revenge on the young man who had stripped him of his fame. Bellini never confessed or even hinted at any involvement, and he died a few years later while performing an act in London, England.

Regardless of how Peer died, the loss of a home-town hero sent Niagara Falls into mourning. Its citizens couldn't believe what had happened. Elgin House Hotel was draped in black crepe, and Peer's body was placed on view. Hundreds came to say goodbye to the "local Blondin" and to view the spot where he fell to his death.

Today, the mystery of Stephen Peer's untimely death still arouses curiosity in readers who come across the story. History records him as the only tightrope walker to die from a fall into the gorge, but no one can agree as to how or why he fell. No new evidence has ever surfaced to support a definitive cause of death, and, as the years pass, the truth recedes farther into the mists of time. More than 120 years later, the mystery remains: accident, murder or suicide?

CHAPTER THREE

Daredevils—Roll out the Barrels

SINCE THE EARLY 1800s, the dream of riches and renown has lured adventurous people into reckless stunts that aim to defy the might of Niagara Falls. The 19th century was dominated by acrobats who crossed the gorge on narrow ropes, divers who leapt from great heights into the river and swimmers who braved the turbulent water. By the 1880s, however, daredevils and those who paid to watch their stunts demanded challenges, new obstacles to overcome. What emerged were risk-takers foolhardy enough to actually go through the roiling waters of Niagara.

At one point or another, thrill seekers have used almost every conceivable contraption—boats, kayaks or various types of self-made vessels—to go through the whirlpool rapids or over the falls, but by far the favored mode of transportation has been the barrel. Something about this kind of craft appealed to riders and audiences alike, something rough and ready and a little more dangerous, even though most barrel-riders made elaborate preparations to ensure their journeys were safe.

The trend began with Carlisle D. Graham who, appropriately enough, was a cooper by trade. On July 11, 1886, he climbed into a barrel specially outfitted with air valves and weighed with ballast and was towed out into the river below the falls. Nine minutes later, having successfully shot the rapids and the whirlpool, he came ashore at Queenston unscathed. Carlisle was willing to share the spotlight and loaned his barrel over the course of that season to several other daredevils, including George Hazlett and Sadie Allen, who became the first male/female team to challenge the rapids at Niagara. In total, 22 barrel trips have been taken through the lower Whirlpool Rapids.

By the early 1900s, however, the rapids no longer posed a challenge. A new century required new thrills, and going over the falls became the obsession for 20th-century barrel-riders. Leading the way was a 63-year-old former schoolteacher, Annie Taylor. To everyone's amazement, she survived the stunt on October 20, 1901, dazed and bloodied but otherwise unharmed. Newspapers hailed her as a heroine, and Annie dubbed herself the "Queen of the Mist." For 10 years, she reigned as the only person to have successfully gone over the falls. No one else dared attempt it.

But although the first thing Annie Taylor said upon emerging from the barrel was "nobody ought ever do that again," it was inevitable that imitators would eventually emerge. Bobby Leach, a circus

George Hazlett and Sadie Allen made a trip together through the Whirlpool Rapids on August 8, 1886. Eyebrows were raised, as they weren't even engaged.

⁓ↄ⅜ⅽↄ⁓

performer, finally matched her feat in 1911. He had already successfully ridden the rapids twice in a barrel in June 1898, but a trip over the falls was to be the pinnacle of his career. He very nearly didn't survive, sustaining serious injuries, including a broken jaw and shattered kneecaps during his ordeal. Yet, heedless of the danger, others followed suit. In total, 16 people have chosen to ride over the falls, five of whom lost their lives in the attempt. These daredevils are considered the elite of Niagara stunters, the bravest of the brave.

Some consider Niagara's barrel-riders to be adventurers who test the limits of human bravery and endurance; others deride them as foolhardy glory-hounds desperate for a few fleeting moments in the limelight. No one can deny, however, that they've provided some of the most dramatic and exhilarating moments in Niagara history.

Maud Willard

Crowds gathered around the Niagara River Whirlpool, breathlessly awaiting the fate of a young woman huddled inside a barrel as it was tossed and tumbled by the raging current of the water. Hour after hour passed, and still the swirling water did not release its grip on the barrel. Concern for the safety of the woman grew more intense among the anxious crowd who, only a short time before, had anticipated watching a never-before attempted Niagara stunt.

Now everyone accepted the harsh truth: Maud Willard's life was obviously in great danger.

Maud Willard was the latest in a string of women who had attempted to find some level of fortune and glory by challenging the might of Niagara. Nothing in her background, however, suggested there was anything of a daredevil in her makeup.

Born in Canton, Ohio, about 30 years earlier, Willard was a burlesque performer, more used to dancing in revealing outfits before hooting crowds of men than to risking her life in foolish stunts. But this woman also had an adventurous side, and, while performing at a Buffalo theater, she was approached by Carlisle Graham with an unusual proposal to join him in an audacious Niagara stunt.

Carlisle Graham was a well-known Niagara daredevil with a series of successful and death-defying performances to his name. Back on July 11, 1886, he had been the first person to shoot the Whirlpool Rapids in a wooden barrel and survive. Since that day, he had repeated the trip four times, including once with his head protruding from the barrel (which left him hard of hearing for the rest of his life). An adoring public called Graham the "Hero of Niagara," a title he felt he had to live up to. As a result, by 1901, he decided to spruce up his tired act, to keep it exciting for his viewers.

What better way to add interest, he thought, than to include a beautiful woman in the act? Graham therefore proposed a double performance with a willing Maud Willard, which, for the first time ever for a Niagara stunt, would be filmed by a movie crew. The Hero of Niagara was greatly admired for his daring and outstanding string of good luck, so Willard must have felt that she was in good hands. Always attracted to a good show and craving the limelight, perhaps even thinking the filmed stunt might lead to better opportunities in show business, she eagerly agreed.

There might have been additional inspiration for Willard. Two days earlier, Martha Wagenfuhrer, a friend of Willard's and a fellow burlesque performer, borrowed Graham's barrel to become the first woman to ride solo through the whirlpool rapids. She emerged badly battered and seasick but otherwise unharmed. Graham convinced Willard to duplicate the feat but with one added twist that would set her apart.

The plan was simple. Willard was going to go through the rapids in Graham's own barrel, the very one in which he had performed his own successful stunts. Graham would wait for her on the American side of the whirlpool. When the barrel emerged from the swirling maelstrom, the Hero of Niagara would dive into the water and swim behind Willard as it continued down the river. Together, they would triumphantly step ashore at Lewiston. The stunt was set for September 7, 1901.

With Martha Wagenfuhrer's success fresh in her memory, Maud Willard probably expected the barrel ride to be a breeze. After all, the barrel, which was solidly built of thick oak, was equipped with air valves, weighted with ballast to ensure it remained right side up and, at 6½ feet long, was comfortable. It had been successfully used half a dozen times already: four times by Graham, once by Wagenfuhrer and once by George Hazlett and

Sadie Allen, who used the barrel in November 1886 to become the first male/female daredevil team to challenge the rapids.

It seemed the barrel was a good luck charm for Carlisle Graham and, indeed, for anyone who used it. Willard had every reason to believe the good fortune would continue with her ride through the rapids. Sadly, her confidence was misplaced. The long string of good luck did not continue with her.

At 3:40 PM on September 7, 1901, the enthusiastic young woman worked her way into the barrel at the *Maid of the Mist* landing. Cradled in her arms was her beloved pet terrier, whose wagging tail suggested it was just as excited about the adventure. The lid of the barrel was secured, and then the barrel was towed out into the middle of the Niagara River, where it was set adrift. Spectators gathered along the river's shores, anxious to see yet another act of bravery.

All eyes were on the barrel as it went under the Whirlpool Rapids Bridge at four o'clock and continued to float along, until it reached the whirlpool itself about five minutes later. As planned, Graham was confidently waiting there for the arrival of the barrel and its passengers. As the barrel came into sight, he put on his life preserver and tied a life ring around his neck to keep his head supported should the waves knock him unconscious.

He waited in anticipation for the barrel to be ejected out of the whirlpool and continue the trip downstream so he could begin his end of the performance. However, the barrel was sucked into the heart of the vortex and held there by the current. Minutes passed, then an hour, and still the whirlpool refused to give up its hold on the barrel. By now the crowd of spectators became worried that a tragedy was about to unfold before their eyes.

Not wanting to disappoint the crowd or the film crew, and with daylight fading, Graham decided to go ahead with his part of the act without Maud. He dove into the water and, half swimming, half riding on the current, raced downstream toward Lewiston. Graham completed his swim without incident and walked back to the whirlpool. He was shocked to see that the barrel was still caught in the raging water, bobbing beyond the reach of rescuers.

Panic had set in among the crowd, especially when, at about five o'clock, the barrel disappeared suddenly below the water's surface. When it resurfaced moments later, it was listing to one side. Many began to worry that Willard had lost consciousness and was slumped over inside. Graham was worried as well and hurried over to the Ontario side of the whirlpool, thinking he might be able to retrieve the barrel from there. By now dusk had fallen, and, in the gathering gloom, Graham frantically swam out in an attempt to bring in the barrel. Despite his best efforts, however, he was unsuccessful, and still the crowd awaited word of Willard's fate.

As darkness settled in, powerful searchlights were trained on the spinning barrel. Hours later, Captain Billy Johnson took over from the exhausted Graham and, using long ropes and life preservers, tried to swim out to the trapped young woman. He, too, failed to rescue Willard. Finally, Archibald Donald, a young man who had recently saved someone from drowning in the whirlpool, swam out and managed to tow the barrel into calmer waters, where others helped bring it to shore.

By this time it was after midnight, and a few of Maud friends had gathered on shore, awaiting her fate. Frantically the lid was ripped off and the rescuers peered inside. They were greeted by Willard's terrier, alive and well, who couldn't wait to be picked up and put on firm ground.

But for Willard's friends and the dozens of spectators who had lingered over the long hours, a dark cloud was cast and their worst fears were confirmed. Maud Willard was dead. Sadly and tragically, it seems her beloved terrier had accidentally killed her by putting its nose into the barrel's only air hole, and by doing so had cut off its owner's air supply, causing her to suffocate. Poor Maud Willard had wanted to share her glory with her best friend. That decision might well have cost her life.

At about 2:00 AM, a number of Maud's friends came to claim her body and bring it up from the water's edge, but a *Toronto Globe* reporter covering the story was not impressed by what he witnessed: "They half carried, half dragged the body of the woman up by her feet and hair," he wrote. "Some were carrying burning embers and torches to light their way: others were falling off the rugged pathways in their drunken stupor as they climbed up the narrow pathway. The worst kind of blasphemy resounded through the glen at the pool and, with flying burning embers before the high wind, presented a weird sight not unlike Dante's Inferno."

Carlisle Graham was devastated by the tragedy and blamed himself for Willard's death. He couldn't escape the reality that it was he who had recruited the young woman to be his partner, never mind that he had no control over the unpredictable waters of the Niagara River and had tried his best to rescue her. As a result of his grieving, Graham refused to attempt anymore stunts through the rapids. Without his daredevil performances to keep him in the public eye, his fame waned, and within a few years, the Hero of Niagara vanished into obscurity.

September 7, 1901, was a sad and tragic day for Niagara residents, a day when a young show girl wanted to put on a performance not to be forgotten. She did just that, but unfortunately the performance was remembered for the loss and not for the daring act she had hoped it would be.

Maud Willard was the first of Niagara's barrel-riders to lose her life in the pursuit of infamy, but unfortunately she wasn't the last.

Queen of the Mist: Annie Taylor

On a warm spring evening in 1921, the "Queen of the Mist" lay in her bed and stared up at the cracks in the ceiling, her fading eyes tracing the lines that seemed to represent the paths her life could have taken. But now, with the strength slipping from her once indomitable body, she saw only the tragic failure she had become. Her mind careened through the events of her life, wondering how it was that the first person to successfully conquer Niagara Falls could be so easily forgotten.

It was a question she couldn't answer and one modern readers will also be hard-pressed to explain. Here was a remarkable woman who, as a senior, no less, decided to ride the falls in a barrel and who, upon plunging over the precipice, created a new and previously unimagined spectacle at Niagara. Annie Taylor had, in her own words, "beat the men at their own game" by one-upping all prior stunts. And yet, she was forgotten only a few short years after her death-defying, history-making experience.

Her story is as spectacular and turbulent as the falls themselves.

Annie Taylor was born in 1838, though no one seems to know the month or day—like so much about the woman, they remain a mystery. She was married at a very young age, but when her doctor husband died while she was still in her late teens, Annie was forced to look after herself. She was, if nothing else, a survivor, and soon became an independent woman. In a day when most women were dependent on men, this self-sufficiency set her apart from the rest of her gender. Annie needed no man.

Annie became a world traveler. She ventured all over North America, visited Cuba and Europe and never really settled down. She supported herself through teaching and was a stern taskmaster in the classroom, a woman with hard features and an even harder sense of discipline.

In 1901, at 63 years of age, Annie was approaching the end of her teaching career. She was desperate to earn enough money for her old age and was perhaps also driven, after a lifetime of serving in a job with few accolades, by a desire to make a name for herself. But how?

Then it came to her. After reading of Carlisle Graham's fifth trip through the Niagara's Whirlpool Rapids on July 15, 1901, Annie impulsively chose to become a Niagara daredevil. Not one to be outdone by men, she decided to become the first person—man or woman—to risk his or her life by going over the falls in a barrel. People were aghast at what seemed like a suicidal act by a woman desperate for attention, but the daring of her plan created widespread interest.

Many of Annie's friends and acquaintances tried desperately to convince her not to go through with her plans, but she was determined and nothing would stop her. Though brave and perhaps reckless, she wasn't foolish, and, rather than risk her life in a standard barrel, she spent $400 of her own money to have a customized barrel built to her specifications. Annie's barrel was made of sturdy and buoyant Kentucky oak and weighed 160 pounds. Inside, a 100-pound iron anvil was supposed to keep the barrel upright in the water.

Annie wanted to be portrayed as a cut above the other daredevils, so under no circumstance would she appear in the outlandish costumes worn by her predecessors, especially the suggestive clothes of the earlier female daredevils. As a woman of refinement, she thought it was unbecoming of someone of her age to parade around in a short skirt. On the day of her trip over the falls, October 24, 1901, she was dressed like a true lady, wearing a long black dress with lacy cuffs and a large black hat. One would think she was dressed for church, rather than a life-endangering voyage over a waterfall.

The brisk fall wind blew a fine mist into the faces of Annie Taylor and the two men, Fred Truesdale and William Holloran, who had been recruited to assist her. Even here, several miles upstream from the falls themselves, the water was frothing and turbulent.

Annie gave the barrel a final look over and then, in her characteristically demanding manner, started to issue orders.

"Now, Fred," she said. "Make sure the photographers are there to take my picture when I emerge from the barrel, and, William, make sure that they don't take my picture until we get a chance to fix my hair."

Both men replied in unison. "Yes, Annie."

The orders continued. "Fred, put that mattress in the barrel. No, not the pillow, that's for my head. The big one, put the big one in first."

"Yes, Annie."

The men did as Annie asked. A down-filled mattress was stuffed into the barrel to cushion her body during the trip, and then, with the assistance of the two men, Annie eased herself in as well. It was cramped and dark inside the barrel, and she found it difficult to shift into a comfortable position. A pillow was passed in for her head, the lid put in place.

"Wait!" Annie's muffled voice echoed from within. "Where's Henry? I can't go without Henry! Give me my baby!"

"Yes, Annie."

The lid was removed, and a tiny, meowing ball of black fur, Annie's beloved kitten, was placed into her outstretched hands. This was the last time the men would see Annie until she surfaced at the bottom of the falls. If she surfaced.

The lid was sealed in place, and the two men nervously jumped into a rowboat to tow the barrel out to the middle of the river. After pumping the last bit of air into the barrel, at 4:05 PM, they cut her loose. "There goes, Annie," the men muttered as the barrel raced through the current.

A crowd had formed around the falls, watching breathlessly as the drama unfolded, turning pale as the barrel and its passengers approached the falls. Many spectators dared not watch as the barrel bucked and lurched closer and closer to the edge and then shot down that awful plunge of 158 feet. The barrel, and Annie and her kitten with it, disappeared behind the enormous cloud of mist that forms at the base of the falls. Some heartless souls wagered that Annie would die before she was recovered, and undoubtedly some men, threatened by the prospect of a woman succeeding where no man had even dared, hoped she would perish.

The silence that draped over the crowd seemed to last forever. The suspense of waiting for Annie to reemerge took its toll on the nerves of one and all. When half an hour passed and there was still no sign of her, the crowd began to despair. And then, suddenly, a mighty cheer that could be heard miles away erupted from the crowd as the barrel miraculously seemed to float away from the mist and came into full view. No one could believe their eyes as the barrel came to a stop near the Canadian shore, bobbing placidly in the shallows of the river. It was 4:40 PM.

Four men in a rowboat grabbed the barrel and hurriedly pried open the lid. Inside, they found Annie, stunned, bleeding and disoriented but still very much alive. One of her rescuers waved to the crowd to signal that she had survived, and a second roar of approval erupted. Dazed from the ordeal, Annie could not find the strength to climb out of the barrel, so the men were forced to saw off the staves to free her.

When at last they lifted her into the boat, Annie, still almost senseless, muttered weakly that "nobody ought to do that again." The spunk she had demonstrated before the stunt was no longer there. The terror of the experience had shaken even the unflappable Annie. Henry, the kitten, was even more terrified, it seemed. When he emerged from the barrel, his downy black fur had turned white as snow.

Annie was later examined by the local doctor, but aside from bruises, bleeding from minor wounds and being in shock, she was uninjured and would in time be fine. Soon after, reporters gathered around to hear about Annie's incredible journey, as she described what the ride was like

Annie Taylor, at the age of 63, became the first person to go over the falls and survive. She emerged shaken but unhurt from the ordeal, though popular legend says her pet cat—who accompanied her on the trip—was so terrified that its black fur turned white.

~❧❧~

inside the barrel, being whirled around at tremendous speed and then crashing into the rocks. When asked if she would ever go over the falls again, Annie shuddered. "If it was with my dying breath,

I would caution anyone against attempting the feat," she said. "I will never go over the falls again. I would sooner walk up to the mouth of a cannon knowing it was going to blow me to pieces than make another trip over the falls."

Newspapers hailed Annie Taylor as a heroine, dubbing her the "Queen of the Mist."

Annie enjoyed her newfound fame, but others profited from it more than she did. The agent she hired to promote her stole the barrel, taking it on a whirlwind tour of the United States and displaying it with a younger and prettier "Annie Taylor." Although Annie herself made a handful of public appearances and wrote an autobiography, she lacked that special touch for public speaking, and so the fortune that she risked her life to achieve never materialized. Within a few years, Annie Taylor, broke and forgotten, became a lonely old woman who dwelled on the memories of her five minutes of fame.

No crowds formed in February 1921 to watch as Annie was admitted to the county poorhouse in Niagara Falls, New York. Nor were they present when she made her final journey two months later, on April 29. Annie died the poor woman she always feared she would become. A collection was taken up to provide her with a decent burial. She rests in Oakwood Cemetery in Niagara Falls, New York.

Two Niagara legends rest alongside each other in death: Carlisle Graham, the first to go through the Whirlpool Rapids in a barrel, and Annie Taylor, the first to survive going over the falls.

Annie Taylor might not have gained the fame or fortune she expected when she risked her life by going over the falls, but 105 years later, her story is still being told. The Queen of the Mist will forever live in our minds as the woman who dared to be a Niagara Falls daredevil.

George Stathakis

George Stathakis, a mysterious figure shrouded in an air of eccentricity, was almost certainly one of the strangest characters to defy the mighty Niagara.

A self-described mystic whose only friend was a turtle he believed was the reincarnation of a divine entity, Stathakis went over the falls in search of metaphysical "truth," not fame or fortune. We'll never know if he found what he sought. He died during the course of his quest for enlightenment.

Before that fateful day in July 1930, when he assured himself a place in the history books with his ill-starred act of daredevilry, George Stathakis was an obscure man of little consequence. Though history records show that he was born in Greece in 1884, he sincerely believed he was born in central Africa 1000 years earlier, on the banks of a river called Abraham. His family was poor but deeply religious, and his education was spotty at best. At some point in his early life, Stathakis began to hear disembodied voices and experience strange visions, which he chalked up to divine inspiration. It was after this development that he created his own complex philosophy that blended religion, pseudo-science, mysticism and fabrication.

In 1910, 26-year-old Stathakis immigrated to the United States and naturally enough became attracted to the spiritualism movement that was sweeping the nation in the early 1900s. Mediums who claimed to gain wisdom from mysterious, unseen forces operated from darkened parlors throughout North America. Mystical beliefs competed with traditional religion; people began to explore the powers of the mind—telepathy and clairvoyance, for example—in an attempt to broaden their understanding of the metaphysical world. It was a time of immense interest in the supernatural.

Stathakis was seduced by this mysterious world and fell deeper and deeper into its fold. What might have been a yearning for faith was the seed that corrupted Stathakis' mind, and the desperation of the Depression provided the fertile soil in which his crazed beliefs took root. In time, he became a hollow spirit bound to a world out of touch with reality. He was so immersed in mysticism and esoteric beliefs that he found it increasingly difficult to keep a job or maintain a relationship. By 1930, he was only occasionally employed in a low-wage job as a chef, and his only real friend was a turtle named Sonny Boy.

Sonny Boy was no mere pet, at least not in Stathakis' deluded eyes. He claimed the turtle was sacred to some obscure Greek cult, was more than 105 years old and quite likely was the avatar of a mysterious god-like entity. Clearly, Stathakis was losing his already tenuous grip on reality. Further evidence of the delusions clouding his mind was his firm belief that he was the first person to stand at the North Pole, where he had proclaimed himself "king and master of the Earth, and from this summit I am going to rule and direct it."

Stathakis' version of his life and his philosophical beliefs were laid out in a book he wrote entitled *The Mysterious Veil of Humanity Through the Ages*.

Much of the book consisted of mystic interviews of the great Greek philosophers Aristotle and Plato, both of whom had been dead for more than 2000 years. Interestingly enough, Stathakis also wrote that he had visited Niagara Falls in the distant past, "at a time when they had not yet been formed."

Yet, Stathakis hardly took note of the pathetic shell his life had become. Friends and jobs were a distraction from his pursuit of enlightenment and truth. He wanted to devote all his free time to spiritual exploration and found such worldly interests as money and relationships of little significance. He wrote several obscure books on the subject, none of which made any sort of impact, but nonetheless with each passing year he felt he was one step closer to his ultimate goal of unlocking the secrets of the universe.

When 1930 rolled around, the increasingly eccentric mystic felt confident he was ready to cross the final threshold into a world beyond our normal understanding. To do that, he would need to take a leap of faith—quite literally, as it turned out.

Stathakis decided to go over Niagara Falls in a barrel. He was sure that the experience would provide mystical insight, that by staring death in the face he would somehow connect with a realm of consciousness only witnessed when leaving this mortal plane. Stathakis had other motives as well, intending to sell the motion picture rights for the stunt to raise the $5000 needed to finance a three-volume book series detailing his spiritual mantra and tracing the history of humankind from its origins to its far future. These books, he hoped, would spread his ideas, create converts and ultimately preserve his name for posterity.

On July 5, 1930, the 46-year-old climbed into a custom-made barrel bobbing in the waters of the Niagara River. The barrel, at 1000 pounds, 10 feet in height, and 5 feet in diameter, was the largest and heaviest barrel yet to test its strength against the power of the falls. At one end was a solid steel cap, and the other had a steel hatch secured with 16 bolts. Stathakis was sure that divine providence was on his side, so he took few precautions beyond padding the interior with a mattress. Into the barrel with him went a pencil and notepad to record his experiences, a tank with a three-hour supply of oxygen and his trusty companion, Sonny Boy.

Just before the lid was nailed shut, Stathakis made a final, prophetic statement to the gathered reporters. "If I die, Sonny Boy will one day reveal the secret of my trip, explaining everything at the proper time." His proclamation might have been mistaken for a joke if his face hadn't been so earnest, his eyes so sincere. The reporters at least had the courtesy to wait until the lid was closed before sharing a chuckle.

The barrel was towed to the head of the rapids at Chippawa, and then, at 3:25 PM, set loose. It raced through the white-capped waters, rising and falling with each wave, hurdling at breakneck speed past thousands of breathless onlookers. Only minutes later, the barrel disappeared over the falls. Eighteen hours passed before it reemerged; during that long, agonizing period, it had been trapped behind the wall of water.

For a time, no one was particularly alarmed. They were certain that at any moment the barrel would appear. But as the three-hour limit of Stathakis' oxygen tank approached, panic spread among the gathered masses. They had come to see a grand spectacle, not a tragic death, and soon enough the mood turned from festive to somber. Sadly, no one could help, as the water behind the falls held the barrel captive, well beyond reach.

By the time the barrel appeared early the next morning, the few remaining onlookers knew George Stathakis would make no triumphant emergence. Boats raced out to retrieve the barrel, and with speed born of desperation, rescuers furiously worked at the bolts that secured the lid. Still, it took several hours to remove the bolts that held the latch in place. Inside the barrel, they found the mystic and would-be conqueror of the falls serene in death. In his cold, blue-tinged hands were the pad of paper and pencil, poised as if about to write. His body had been undamaged by the 177-foot drop, leaving the coroner to conclude that Stathakis had suffocated when his oxygen ran out.

Did Stathakis find truth, meaning or some mystical insight before he left our world? We'll never know. But if he did, he certainly didn't record it—the paper he had brought with him in the barrel was blank. Which leads to a question that has mystified people for nearly a century now: Why hadn't Stathakis written something, a final parting message, some insight, even an epitaph of sorts, before his oxygen ran out? Surely, as the oxygen within the barrel thinned, he must have realized that death was waiting near at hand to wrap him in its cold embrace. And yet he made no attempt to say goodbye. It was almost as if he wanted to remain a conundrum for all eternity.

Stathakis' tragic story doesn't end there. His body lay in the county morgue for several weeks, waiting for someone—anyone—to claim it, but no one ever did. He had led such a reclusive life that no friend or family came forward. Such was the depths to which his personal fortunes had sunk, and as a result, he was buried in a pauper's grave in Niagara Falls, unmourned and quickly forgotten.

Unlike its owner, Sonny Boy survived the trip over the falls. The turtle's adventures were just beginning, however. River man "Red" Hill exhibited the sacred turtle and Stathakis' barrel in a tent behind the Lafayette Hotel. A few days after the tragic episode, the hapless reptile was kidnapped. Some said the culprit was a mystic eager to claim the turtle's power as his own, though saner heads suggested the individual responsible simply hoped to profit financially by putting the animal on exhibit. Sonny Boy was eventually recovered, but, despite its owner's predictions, never spoke nor shared any insight into exactly what transpired during those terrifying hours trapped within the barrel.

As a result, Stathakis went to the grave as he lived, a complete enigma.

The barrel that cost the eccentric his life, the so-called Death Barrel, lies within the IMAX Theatre in Niagara Falls as part of its free display of daredevil paraphernalia—incidentally, the largest collection of original daredevil barrels anywhere. It is a somber reminder that death, far more so than fame or fortune, or even truth, was often the only reward for those who thought they could tame the mighty Niagara.

CHAPTER FOUR

The Stars Come to Niagara

OVER THE YEARS, MANY famous people have been among the 15 million annual visitors to Niagara Falls. They often sneak into town with little fanfare and slip out almost unnoticed. Other times, celebrities arrive with more publicity, temporarily—and sometimes unintentionally—detracting attention away from the falls and onto themselves. The most famous example of this was the 1953 visit by Hollywood starlet Marilyn Monroe, to film the movie *Niagara*. For three weeks, the natural beauty of the falls played second fiddle to the glamour and presence of one of the most attractive women to ever grace the silver screen.

The first person of fame to visit Niagara Falls was the Duke of Kent, father of Queen Victoria of Great Britain, who came in 1791. Since then, almost every member of the royal family, from Queen Elizabeth and her sister, Princess Margaret, to Princess Diana and her two young sons, has made the pilgrimage to Niagara Falls. It's almost a royal tradition. The notable exception to this is Queen Victoria; despite living until the age of 93, she never made the trip.

Almost every American president since James Madison in 1817 has similarly made time to take in the falls. Abraham Lincoln, arguably the greatest U.S. president of all, visited the region several times during the 1850s before being elected to the White House. Jimmy Carter spent his 50th wedding anniversary in Niagara Falls, Ontario, in 1996. Other statesmen who've made official visits to the falls include British Prime Minister Winston Churchill, who came in 1943 while planning the strategy of World War II with his American allies; Indian Prime Minister Indira Gandhi; Soviet Premier Mikhail Gorbachev; and Pope John Paul II, who visited in 1978, when he was Archbishop of Krakow in Poland and still known as Karol Cardinal Wojtylka.

Many celebrated authors have sought inspiration at the falls. Not all were successful. Harriet Beecher Stowe's 1834 visit left her in awe and wonder. "Oh, it is lovelier than it is great," she wrote, "...so veiled in beauty that we gaze without terror...." Charles Dickens was similarly impressed: "Niagara was at once stamped upon my heart," he exulted, "an image of beauty." However, Oscar Wilde, a noted cynic, had a different opinion: "Every American bride is taken there, and the sight must be one of the earliest, if not the keenest disappointments in American married life."

And, of course, many Hollywood stars have come to witness the great natural wonder. The list includes Jimmy Stewart, Shirley Temple, Gene Autry, Ginger Rogers and countless others. Yet, aside from Marilyn Monroe's *Niagara,* surprisingly few movies have taken advantage of the stunning scenery by filming at the falls. The most notable, however, was the 1979 film *Superman,* in which the superheroic Man of Steel (played by Christopher Reeve) rescues trouble-prone reporter Lois Lane (Margot Kidder) from a near-fatal plunge over the falls.

The roar and hiss of the rapids, the beauty and danger of the mist-veiled cataract, the many attractions of the region—it doesn't matter if you're rich or poor, famous or anonymous, the majesty of Niagara Falls is an irresistible lure to all humanity.

Jimmy Stewart

Awkward yet charming, modest yet successful, quiet yet courageous, actor James "Jimmy" Stewart embodied America at its best. Yet, when he visited Niagara Falls in the fall of 1940, Canadian fans embraced him as one of their own. His was the most celebrated visit of a movie star to date, and for two days the falls took second place to a budding Hollywood icon.

James Stewart was born in small-town Pennsylvania in 1908 and initially had no aspirations to stardom. Instead, he studied architecture at university and only considered his theater experiences while there an amusing pastime. Fate had other plans in store for the unassuming young man, however. He was discovered by a Hollywood gossip columnist, who touted his naturalness and obvious ability to MGM studios. Soon, Stewart had a screen test and was signed to a contract, and in 1935, he made his first film appearance. By 1939, with a string of hits that included *Vivacious Lady* (1938), *The Shopworn Angel* (1938), *You Can't Take It With You* (1938) and *Mr. Smith Goes to Washington* (1939), Stewart had solidified his position as one of the most bankable young stars in Tinseltown.

Determined to make the most of their asset, MGM cast Stewart in three more films in 1940: *The Shop Around the Corner, The Mortal Storm* and *The Philadelphia Story,* for which he won his one and only Oscar for best actor. Each of the films was a hit, but the grueling schedule over the intervening years left Stewart exhausted physically and emotionally. He was ground down by the demands of Hollywood and needed a break from the cameras and the stress of having to carry a film. Jimmy Stewart needed a vacation.

Determined to get as far away from the Hollywood lifestyle as possible, Stewart avoided the hot spots of the rich and famous and instead decided to head for the unspoiled wilderness of Lake Temagami, in northern Ontario. Unmarried at the time, he invited his parents and two sisters along for two weeks of fishing and hiking. There were no frills and whistles, only modest food and accommodations, and perks were in the form not of attentive service nor complementary gifts but rather endless solitude, fresh air and a refreshing simplicity to life. The time off rejuvenated Stewart, and he was greatly impressed with the rugged beauty of the area.

On the way home, the Stewarts paid a visit to Niagara Falls on September 6 and 7, booking rooms at the General Brock Hotel (now Crowne Plaza Hotel). The General Brock was the place to stay in Niagara. Built in 1927 for the then-astronomical cost of $1.5 million, it was the first luxury hotel in the area and, due in part to its elegant ballroom and rooftop garden, was at the time considered among the most majestic and celebrated hotels in Ontario. At the hotel's opening, the *Niagara Falls Review* raved that it was, "gleaming white in the sunshine, classic in appearance, looming over the Niagara River," and was without question "the last word in comfort and beauty."

Guests who stayed at the General Brock during its golden years included Walt Disney, Shirley Temple, Marilyn Monroe, Gene Autry and a young Queen Elizabeth and Princess Margaret. Although the ledger boasted many recognizable names, Jimmy Stewart was the first big-name celebrity to enjoy the hospitality of the fine hotel.

Stewart's impending arrival at the General Brock Hotel was the worst-kept secret around, and it wasn't long before word of his visit spread all over Niagara Falls. The result was that when the actor arrived to check in, a large crowd of eager autograph seekers was there to meet him. Though on vacation and badly in need of escape from the demands of stardom, Stewart was gracious with the fans and lingered to sign autographs. Such affability was typical of the man and was undeniably part of his charm. Few fans left disappointed.

Later that day, Stewart and his family viewed the falls and toured along the Niagara River. He was like any other tourist, taking photographs, marveling at the sights, asking questions. Stewart was delighted with what he saw, later telling a reporter that he thought the falls were "the most picturesque sight he had ever seen." The awestruck actor was also "thrilled to death" with the scenery along the river. That evening, Stewart and his family were dinner guests of the General Brock's manager, Ronald Peck, and his wife. During the course of the evening, the party ventured up to the rooftop garden to enjoy the panorama. At 10 stories in height, the General Brock was a Niagara Falls skyscraper for its day, so the view was the best in town.

The following morning, as the Stewarts stepped out of the hotel elevator, they were greeted by a *Niagara Falls Review* reporter who, to his astonishment, "received a warm and cordial welcome from the family." Stewart further surprised the reporter by granting him time for a rather lengthy, if informal, interview. Clearly, James Stewart was no ordinary Hollywood star.

The *Review* reporter discovered that Stewart's reputation for his easy charm and down-to-earth manner wasn't misplaced. "Mr. Stewart is a modest chap," wrote the impressed journalist. "He refuses to discuss his success in pictures and does not make out to be different than any ordinary person. An interesting point about him is his desire to stand and chat with admirers."

When asked about his own favorite actors and actresses, Stewart suggested that Spencer Tracy and Margaret Sullivan were, in his opinion, "superior to any in Hollywood."

When the interview was over, Stewart found the hotel entrance once again crowded with fans eager for a chance to see their idol and perhaps gain an autograph. There were dozens of them, each one demanding a piece of the star's attention, and yet the unflappable star took it all in stride, lingering long enough to send most of his fans home happy with a signature or the memory of a brief conversation with a screen legend.

Later that day, Jimmy Stewart and his family left Niagara Falls to return home to the United States. The Canadian vacation, short though it was, reinvigorated Stewart and gave him the energy and passion to film three more movies in 1941. These were his final films for more than five years, because, in the immediate aftermath of the Japanese bombing of Pearl Harbor on December 7, 1941, Stewart enlisted for service in World War II.

While he was flying bomber missions over Germany (a total of 20, becoming decorated in the process), many of his acting brothers remained in the lap of luxury in Hollywood, having opted out of military duty. Once again, Stewart proved he was hardly the typical Hollywood star.

It was this down-to-earth, everyman persona that made Jimmy Stewart such a hit with the people during his two days in Niagara Falls in 1940. Unlike other stars, who demanded special treatment and saw the sights surrounded by a screen of heavy protection or under a shroud of secrecy, Stewart was approachable and accommodating. As a result, hundreds of Niagara residents were left with warm memories of having seen and met one of Hollywood's greatest treasures.

Shirley Temple

When we're young, many of us dream of being a star, but few of us ever become famous. For Shirley Temple, the dream became a reality at the very young age of three, when she made her film appearance in 1931. As an adorable child star, she represented the possibility that dreams could indeed come true, and, as a result, she gave hope and cheer to people during the long years of the Great Depression.

Shirley Temple was one of Hollywood's most famous celebrities throughout the 1930s and '40s. Loved by both the young and young-at-heart, she was voted as the number one movie star in the

United States. But she didn't just belong to Americans; Shirley Temple was adored in Canada as well and nowhere more so than in Niagara Falls, where her 1944 visit served as a beacon of light during the dark days of World War II.

Born in 1928 and blessed with uncommon talent as an actress, singer and dancer, Temple began making short comedies in the early 1930s. By 1932, she was making as many as four films per year, movies that were watched by millions across the world, and every girl looked to her for inspiration. Shirley Temple was a household name. *Bright Eyes*, a film created especially for her and released in 1934, cemented her status as a box-office star and featured her most famous song, "On the Good Ship Lollipop," which every child in America was soon singing.

With her famous blonde ringlets, cute dimples and sunny disposition, she charmed and entertained theater audiences during the Depression years. Her singing and dancing captivated millions and helped to raise people's spirits during a difficult period. In fact, she was so essential to public morale during this time that President Franklin Roosevelt famously remarked, "As long as we have Shirley Temple, we'll be alright." The hopes of an entire nation rested on the tiny shoulders of a young child.

Just when America was beginning to emerge from the Depression, Shirley Temple's magic seemed to fade. She was no longer a precious little girl, and her films began to suffer at the box office. Although Shirley continued to make movies until her teens in the 1940s, none again catapulted her to the pinnacle of Hollywood.

Stardom was of little concern to Shirley at the time. World War II was raging, and with two brothers in the United States Marine Corps, the teenager concentrated more on raising wartime morale than acting. Millions of servicemen in the U.S. and Canada had literally grown up watching her and, indeed, alongside her, so she was immensely popular with young soldiers and sailors. Her weekly mail ran into the thousands, most of it from servicemen who saw her as their kid sister. Shirley returned their affection, often visiting wounded men in hospitals to keep their spirits up and making appearances at military bases, where she chatted and danced with the men.

It was in this goodwill capacity, during October 1944 and while World War II was still raging, that Shirley Temple graced Canada with her presence. Her first stop was the nation's capital, Ottawa, where she was scheduled for several appearances to help promote the sale of war bonds. It was believed that the presence of a movie star would encourage people to come out and generously support this important cause.

While in Ottawa, Shirley had a private conversation with Prime Minister W.L. Mackenzie King, during which she learned he was a spiritualist, who, he claimed, was in frequent contact with his dead mother.

On Sunday, October 22, 1944, Shirley, accompanied by her parents and publicity agent, arrived by train in Niagara Falls, Ontario, to participate in more charitable work. Once settled in the General Brock Hotel, she was taken around the area to see the various Niagara attractions. Escorted by George Inglis, Niagara Falls' mayor at the time, the 16-year-old enjoyed the sights along the Niagara River, including the famous Spanish Aero Car, which she felt was "quite impressive."

She also visited Oak Hall, which was being used as an RCAF (Royal Canadian Air Force) Convalescent Home. For the ill and wounded airmen, seeing the young actress in person and getting the opportunity to speak with her was a treat that certainly must have lifted their spirits.

Shirley Temple was then taken to the residence of Fred Cairns for tea. Cairns was an important figure in the community and the manager of Borden's Dairy. Cairns and his wife, Tillie, lived in an elegant, two-story house, where the young Hollywood star apparently felt quite at home—so much so, in fact, that when the doorbell rang and her hostess did not hear it, Shirley pleasantly got up to greet the visitor.

America's sweetheart, Shirley Temple, became Canada's object of affection for a few days in 1944. While in Niagara, she visited all the usual sights but also enjoyed tea and a quiet afternoon away from the spotlight in this private residence.

~⋅⊃⋅⊂⋅~

During her tea with the Cairns, Shirley confided that even though it would be a long time before she got married, when she did, "it would be a toss-up between here and Hawaii for my honeymoon." She went on to elaborate on how struck she was by Niagara's beauty. As it turned out, however, Shirley married twice, but on neither occasion did she spend her honeymoon at Niagara Falls.

Following the tea, Shirley Temple was driven to Queen Victoria Park, where a huge crowd anxiously awaited her arrival. A reporter noted she was wearing "a smart black jersey dress with jet black buttons under a mink coat, and a black hat over her golden hair." The crowd went wild when the young star greeted them with a wave of her hand and a warm smile. She was to be the guest of honor in a ceremony that had two purposes: raising funds through Victory Bonds to support the war and the resumption of the falls being illuminated.

The relighting of the falls was an important event for the residents of Niagara Falls. Permanent illumination of the falls had started in 1925, and this nightly tradition became extremely popular and a source of pride for locals. Since the start of World War II in 1939, however, the lights had been turned off to conserve electricity for war production purposes. It was a heartbreaking development for many locals; they understood the need for sacrifice, but seeing the falls cast in darkness each night seemed to represent the fortunes of the country as it struggled through years of defeat at the hands of Nazi Germany. But, by October 1944, with victory close at hand, it was decided that the falls could once again be regularly illuminated. The ceremony symbolized a slow return to normalcy and was therefore greeted with an outpouring of emotion. The presence of Shirley Temple helped to make that day a truly memorable and significant historical occasion.

Among the large crowd that night were two young Air Force men, who managed to strike up a conversation with Shirley and summon the courage to ask for her autograph. While chatting, the men happened to mention that they were about to hitchhike to Hamilton when the lighting ceremony was over.

Shirley realized she was going to the same city to catch a train to Chicago, so she graciously offered the two surprised men a ride. Naturally, they didn't pass up an invitation as wonderful as that! To have the pleasure of traveling with Shirley Temple was an experience of a lifetime, and they enthusiastically accepted her offer.

It's doubtful these young men ever forgot Shirley Temple's time in Niagara Falls. In general, though, her brief visit to the community is rarely remembered, a mere footnote in the long history of the area. But we will never forget the way she stole our hearts and entertained us with her charm, and even today you can be sure that somewhere, someone's young child is watching one of her timeless movies.

Marilyn Monroe

The legend of Marilyn Monroe is as strong today as it was decades ago, even though most of today's fans weren't even born when the Hollywood starlet died. Her popularity, her legend, is without a doubt stronger in death than it was in life. She will be remembered forever as a beautiful young woman.

Growing up, however, Marilyn was filled with insecurities and unhappiness. Her upbringing was far from pleasant; it was in fact a grim and difficult experience that left her emotionally scarred for life. She was born Norma Jean Mortensen but was later baptized Norma Jean Baker, for her single mother Gladys Baker. Gladys, whose family had a history of mental illness, had a breakdown and was hospitalized for a short time after giving birth to Norma Jean. Gladys never recovered (in fact, she suffered from mental illness until her death in 1984) and wasn't able to be a mother to Norma Jean.

The young Norma Jean spent her life being shuffled from orphanage to orphanage, never feeling wanted or secure. When Norma Jean was 16, her guardian, to avoid sending her to another orphanage, arranged for her to marry a man named Jim Dougherty, who was five years Norma's senior. Reluctantly, Norma Jean agreed.

The marriage was predictably short-lived, enduring only two troubled years. With her husband in the merchant marine during World War II, Norma Jean worked in a factory stuffing parachutes. This is where her story really starts. She caught the eye of a photographer, who believed she would make an excellent model, and, on the basis of his encouragement, Norma Jean left her life, her hometown and her husband behind. With her dark hair now bleached blonde, a studio contract in hand and

For two weeks in 1952, the Niagara Falls had to share the spotlight with another natural beauty, Hollywood starlet Marilyn Monroe, here shooting her biggest hit, the film *Niagara*.

a new name, Marilyn Monroe, the original Blonde Bombshell, was born.

Marilyn Monroe's acting career soon took off, with such movies as *Scudda Hoo! Scudda Hay!* (1947), *Dangerous Years* (1948) and *Ladies of the Chorus* (1948). But the release of *Gentlemen Prefer Blondes* in 1953 was when Marilyn truly became noticed. Her sex appeal captivated men, and young women dreamed of being like her. And her appeal wasn't limited to the United States. She was beloved in Canada as well and never more so than when Hollywood and Twentieth Century-Fox came to Niagara Falls, Canada, to film Marilyn's latest movie.

It was big news at the time. For about two weeks during June 1952, Niagara Falls had an extra attraction beyond the raging falls themselves, and residents and visitors delighted at the news that one of Hollywood's blonde beauties was in their midst. *Niagara*, the vision of Hollywood screenwriter and producer Charles Brackett, was coming to life.

Brackett had visited Niagara Falls, Ontario, in the fall of 1951 and fell in love with the scenery. He envisioned a movie starring Marilyn Monroe, in what was to be her first starring role, and took full advantage of the magical setting. Brackett made sure to use many of the local Niagara Falls landmarks in the film, including City Hall, the old post office at the corner of Park and Zimmerman, the bus depot (which at the time was located at the Rainbow Bridge), the hospital (then on Jepson Street) and the village of Chippawa.

But Niagara Falls, attractive as it is, didn't have everything the filmmaker required to make his dream a reality. The script called for a motel overlooking the falls, but there simply wasn't one, because Queen Victoria Park occupied all of the lands along the river's shore. As a result, a makeshift motel was constructed in the park, directly opposite the American Falls and with a view toward the Horseshoe Falls. Named the

Rainbow Motel, the six-unit building (most of which was false-fronted) was built by local contractor Arthur Jolley and was the setting for many of the most important scenes of the movie.

The false motel garnered a great deal of attention from the public, many of whom thought it was real. As the *Niagara Falls Review* noted in its edition of June 5, 1952, "Thousands of people visited Queen Victoria Park yesterday and today, but nary a glance did they cast towards the mighty cataracts. All attention was focused on the 'Rainbow Motel' where Twentieth Century-Fox was shooting scenes for the full-length technicolour film Niagara."

Unlike the comedies that had dominated most of Marilyn Monroe's career, *Niagara* was a dark suspense drama that co-starred Joseph Cotton and Jean Peters and also featured Casey Adams, Lurene Tuttle and Jack Benny's announcer of many years, Don Wilson. Along with the cast were about 50 crewmembers for this production, which had a price tag of $2 million, a considerable amount of money at that time.

The film was very much a local production—many residents had the thrill of being hired as behind-the-scenes workers, and 300 Niagara residents, mostly from amateur drama groups, garnered roles as extras (actors with small roles), some of whom shared scenes—if only in a minor way—with Marilyn herself.

Though all of the film's stars naturally received a lot of attention from the public while in town, the main focus was on the Blonde Beauty herself, who arrived on June 5, three days after filming had begun. Marilyn was often greeted by huge crowds wherever she went, but director Henry Hathaway sternly kept her away from the public for fear of distraction. For most of the 13 days of filming, Marilyn was kept on a fairly short leash.

But it wasn't all work and no play for Marilyn Monroe during her time at Niagara Falls. She did a bit of sightseeing that included strolling through Queen Victoria Park, shopping at the Table Rock Gift Shop, taking trips to Niagara-on-the-Lake with then-boyfriend and baseball star Joe DiMaggio and an impromptu ride on the *Maid of the Mist*. One of the most memorable events for Marilyn might have been her trip to the Oneida Company, during which she toured the former silverware plant. After the visit, the star was given a complete set of the "White Orchid" pattern silverware from the company's new collection that was to be released to the general public in the fall of that year. The plant was located where the new Casino Niagara is now.

Marilyn stayed at the exclusive General Brock Hotel in room 801. The rest of the cast stayed in the hotel as well, though most of the crew had more modest accommodations at area motels.

Filming wrapped on June 18. Before leaving, Henry Hathaway expressed his thanks to the residents and business people of Niagara Falls for their hospitality and cooperation. The *Niagara Falls Review* reported that he went on to say, "everyone has been extremely kind and cordial to all of us. We have enjoyed our brief stay here and return home with memories of a gracious community and beautiful country." Marilyn shared the sentiment; she found the people friendly and willing to answer her many questions about the falls, and she enjoyed her limited opportunities to explore the region.

While in Niagara, Marilyn somehow managed to juggle two relationships between takes. One of her suitors, Joe DiMaggio, stayed on the American side in Hotel Niagara but slipped across to rendezvous with her several times a week. At the same time, Marilyn was growing close to her long-time friend Bob Slatzer, and the two shared adjoining rooms. With the falls as a stunning backdrop, Slatzer proposed to Marilyn, and she tearfully accepted. The magic of Niagara did not endure, however. The couple married in Tijuana, Mexico, on June 18 and were divorced just four days later.

But none of Marilyn's personal drama was known to her adoring fans, who eagerly awaited the arrival of *Niagara* in theaters. The world premiere was shown simultaneously at Niagara Falls, Ontario, and Niagara Falls, New York, on

January 28, 1953. More than 200 local dignitaries were at the event, though none of the movie's stars attended. Most chose to attend the New York premiere held two weeks later.

In Niagara Falls, Ontario, the film was shown at the Seneca Theatre, and despite a seating capacity of more than 1000, the demand was so great the movie had to be shown five times per day for more than a week. In the end, *Niagara* was one of the biggest movies of 1953 and catapulted Marilyn Monroe to stardom.

The movie also helped cement Niagara Falls' reputation as the Honeymoon Capital of the World. For years, the local Chamber of Commerce had received hundreds of letters from people inquiring about rooms at the Rainbow Motel featured in the movie. Of course, the Rainbow Motel did not exist; the set had been hastily torn down as soon as filming was completed.

The film also left a lasting impression with many of Niagara's residents, who later recalled their memories with writer George Bailey for his book, *Marilyn Monroe and the Making of Niagara*. Barbara Thompson, who was four months pregnant at the time, had a chance to speak with Marilyn between her scenes. She recalled Marilyn saying, when she was called back for another take, that "She had to go again and be sexy."

And yes, Marilyn was sexy. Her walk, her talk and her mannerisms were all intoxicating for men. But was this really Marilyn Monroe, or was she simply being what Hollywood expected of a Blonde Bombshell? We would never really find out; 10 years and two months after *Niagara* was filmed, Marilyn was found dead in her Hollywood home, and the world mourned her loss.

Not many people would remember Marilyn's brief time in Niagara Falls, and even *Niagara* is overshadowed by some of her more famous films, but we will never forget the legend of the blonde beauty who captivated our hearts with her movies and led a troubled life that was tragically cut short.

Marilyn Monroe was quoted as saying: "Sometimes I think it would be easier to avoid old age, to die young, but then you'd never complete your life, would you?"

Marilyn did indeed die young, and we'll never know how the remainder of her life would have turned out. But we'll always have *Niagara* to remember her by.

Princess Diana

HOW DO YOU TRULY say goodbye to a woman you hardly knew and yet oddly felt was a part of your own life? How do you express your grief, especially when the death is sudden and tragic?

These were questions many were left to ponder on that tear-filled day when the woman known to many as "England's Rose" left this world.

It was early in the morning of August 31, 1997, when the news traveled across the world that Diana, the Princess of Wales, had been in a terrible car accident while visiting Paris. For a time, the people huddled around their televisions dared to hope that she would survive, that the stories circulating about the extent of her injuries were grossly exaggerated. But then word emerged that Diana had succumbed to her extensive injuries and died. The world went into mourning.

That summer, people from seemingly every nation cried in disbelief for a woman, a mother and a new type of royal—elegant and yet all-too human—who had captivated their hearts from the first day the cameras captured her innocent smile.

Born Lady Diana Spencer on July 1, 1961, she was barely 19 years old when Prince Charles, heir to the throne of England, stole her heart. Lady Diana and Prince Charles were married on July 29, 1981, in a fairytale wedding at St. Paul's Cathedral in London. The ceremony was televised live to a worldwide audience of 750 million.

Few people would have recognized Lady Diana before that moment; she was shy and quiet, shunning publicity. But after the wedding, everyone felt they knew her, and soon they fell in love with her.

Young girls were inspired by Diana. Every girl's dream, after all, is to live a fairytale, and as a result of the magical nuptials, Princess Diana had demonstrated to young women everywhere that sometimes dreams really do come true.

Adults were no less taken with her. Princess Diana's natural charm, flair, compassion, beauty and wit were all complemented by a winning smile that made her one of the most dazzling personalities of the time. People were fascinated by her, and, as a result, she became one of the most written about and photographed women of the 20th century.

But it didn't matter how many people loved Princess Diana, her heart belonged to the two greatest gifts she had been given: her two boys.

The royal couple, Prince Charles and Princess Diana, was blessed with two heirs to the throne. The eldest and future king, Prince William, was born in June 1982. Prince Harry arrived two years later. For Princess Diana, being a good mother to her two sons was the meaning of life, the purpose for her existence. Even as her fairytale marriage was unraveling, she and the young princes found happiness with one another. She took them everywhere, hoping to nurture their growth and expand their horizons beyond the protective walls that typically surrounded members of royalty.

Throughout her reign as princess, Lady Diana visited many countries and cherished each for their uniqueness. Canada, it was said, always held a special place in her heart. Perhaps that was the result of fond memories of time spent with her children at Niagara Falls in 1991.

Princess Diana's itinerary was hectic wherever she went, but when she and Prince Charles made a trip to Canada that autumn with the two princes in hand, she made sure to find an opportunity to experience Niagara Falls. So, while Charles remained in Toronto on business, she and her sons took a short helicopter ride south to Canada's greatest natural wonder.

At 11:30 AM on Saturday, October 26, they arrived in Niagara. A heavy mist was blowing over the area as the royals were driven to the first destination of their trip, Table Rock. Here they would get a great view of the falls. Princes William and Harry were obviously excited, and, acting as any child would, ran back and forth between the binocular viewers to get an even closer look at the falls. They'd never seen anything like this, and with their mother and a crowd of dignitaries and officials hovering protectively nearby, the boys climbed the railings to get as close to the thundering spectacle as safety allowed.

The miserable weather did not put a damper on their visit; in fact, the wet conditions didn't seem to bother the boys one bit. William was heard saying, "I think it's lovely, I don't mind the mist at all."

Princess Diana was proud of her sons and would have done anything for them. Seeing her little princes enjoying themselves, acting like children instead of royalty, was all she could ask for. She so wanted them to have some sort of a normal life and enjoy their childhood.

Suddenly the mist let up, allowing a little sun to break through. At this point, Diana, radiant despite being cold and chilled by dampness, walked over to the thousand or so spectators crowding nearby. To their delight, not only did she speak to them pleasantly and intimately, but she also extended her hand in a gesture of warmth. Lady Diana glowed with obvious pride when she turned back to witness her young sons doing the same thing.

After spending considerable time greeting the public, the royals enjoyed an exploration of the caves that make up the Journey Behind the Falls attraction. And of course, every visitor to Niagara looks forward to a voyage on the *Maid of the Mist*, so they also squeezed that into the busy agenda for the day. In fact, the best-remembered image of their short visit to Niagara was a photograph of the three royals as they donned the blue waterproof coats provided to all passengers on the tour boat.

The journey on the *Maid* was probably the highlight of the day for Princes William and Harry.

They were escorted to the ship's bridge, where both took turns as skipper, handling the wheel and blowing the horn. It was any little boy's dream come true. Even Princess Diana took a brief turn at the helm. From the upper deck, the boys waved to the crowds that had gathered along the banks of the gorge in an attempt to get another look at the royals. Princess Diana was visibly pleased that her sons were enjoying their trip and had inherited her "common touch" with the people.

Lunch was spent in the Commissioner's Quarters of the Victoria Park Restaurant. The princes demonstrated the humility Diana instilled in them by clearing their own plates from the table. With their three-hour tour of Niagara coming to an end, Princess Diana and her boys boarded the helicopter and returned to Toronto to be reunited with Prince Charles.

Having the opportunity to see Princess Diana and her two sons was a thrill for many Niagara residents. The excitement it generated was only matched by the visit of another much beloved beauty decades earlier, Marilyn Monroe. Eerily, Princess Diana and the Hollywood starlet, both of whom were remembered as much for the tragedy of their deaths as for their luminous lives, had a great deal in common. Both had their lives cut short, dying at age 36. Both died under mysterious circumstances that led conspiracy theorists to cry bloody murder. Both were honored by Elton John with the song "Candle in the Wind" (he originally wrote it for Marilyn Monroe, and then rewrote the words for Princess Diana). And both women will be eternally young and beautiful.

But such comparisons were for the future, in the sad hours after Princess Diana was pronounced dead. In the late autumn of 1991, residents of Niagara basked in the excitement of the royal visit. Most who met Princess Diana were impressed not so much with her elegance and charm but with her genuineness.

For those fortunate enough to see the royals, it was a day they never forgot, a cherished memory. But one wonders whether Princes William and Harry view their trip to the falls with their mother in the same light. Memories can be embedded in one's mind for a lifetime, and with the untimely death of Princess Diana, perhaps that's all William and Harry have left of their mother. One hopes they find some solace when looking back to that day in October 1991—a day when all three seemed perfectly content and blissfully happy.

Diana will always be the People's Princess, but, more importantly, she will be remembered as a mother who adored her sons. And never was that love more evident than during their three hours in Niagara Falls.

❧✕❧

CHAPTER FIVE

Disasters and Heroic Rescues

THE NIAGARA RIVER IS awe-inspiring in its primal power, violence and unpredictability. Whereas perhaps 100 people have dared to pit themselves against the roaring waters during one headline-grabbing stunt or another, the number who unwillingly find themselves in a life-or-death battle against the forces of nature is many times that. In these terrifying moments of crisis, no fame or glory is to be had, and only thoughts of survival remain. All too often, nature wins; rarely has a year gone by when the Niagara did not claim a life—or multiple lives—in dramatic fashion.

The list of disasters that have occurred in Niagara Falls over the past 200 years is frightening in its grim variety. As well as shipwrecks and groundings in the river, on occasion, boats find themselves trapped by the current and pulled through the tempestuous water. Extremes of weather have destroyed even the most well-built structures. Great fires devastated buildings, ruining businesses and leaving innocents dead or homeless. Train wrecks and collapsing bridges became the painful impetus for change.

During the 19th century, when engineering methods were relatively primitive and regulations were all but nonexistent, disasters of one form or another were nearly routine. As we progressed into the 1900s, and marked improvement in technology and safety regulations occurred, there was real optimism that these tragic incidents were now a thing of the past. Unfortunately, such optimism was unfounded. Despite all our advances, nature retains its power to wreak havoc, and it becomes apparent that humans are not impervious to mishap or disaster.

Sometimes the tragedies in Niagara served as painful lessons that ultimately led to important changes. In 1910, for example, a car of the Great Gorge Route electric railway fell down the embankment and into the rapids. Twelve died. Seven years later, heavy rains washed out a section of the rail bed, causing cars to once again fall into the river. More than 60 died. In light of these incidents, and others like them, it was eventually decided to close the trolley route. Similarly, at one time, it was all the rage to venture onto the ice bridge that forms below the falls, but after several people drowned during a sudden breakup in 1912, the practice was forbidden. The trauma shocked people into action so that more lives were not lost.

But whereas the stories of these varied disasters focus on the grim loss of life, more fascinating is the manner in which people respond in times of crisis. Only when faced with imminent death is the true nature of the human spirit revealed. In many cases, people rise to the challenge, bravely facing the danger and even putting their lives at risk to assist others. Because of the courage and selflessness of humans, potential disasters have been averted and daring rescues pulled off that saved people from the jaws of death.

While we as a people show remarkable resiliency in moving on after painful episodes, we seem unable to forget the grim moments and the human cost. Perhaps that's how it should be. One thing is absolutely certain: Niagara Falls' disasters and heroic rescues provide some of the most compelling moments in the area's long history.

Death on the Ice Bridge

He held her close and looked into her eyes with all the love in his heart. He felt weak and helpless; he could do nothing to save their lives. He would have willingly sacrificed himself if it meant his wife could live, but that wasn't an option. Gently wiping the tears from her eyes, he caressed her face and gave her a long, loving kiss as both slipped into the depths of the icy water and to their deaths.

Eldridge Stanton, 36, and his wife Clara, 28, were like any young couple in love. They enjoyed each other's company, the simple pleasure of strolling hand in hand, and the chance to experience someplace new together. Niagara Falls, then as now, is a magical place in the winter, with gorgeous snow-shrouded scenery that transforms it into a different world than the one summer tourists see. With this in mind, it should come as no surprise that the two lovebirds, Eldridge and Clara, decided on a midwinter visit.

Hands joined, they walked out onto the ice bridge, a frozen sheet below the falls, stretching from shore to shore, that allowed people the opportunity to venture out onto the river and view Mother Nature's spectacular creation in a whole new light. The couple smiled at one another, anticipating a blissful morning together.

It was Sunday, February 4, 1912, a bright and clear day, though windy and bitterly cold. Eldridge and Clara Stanton couldn't have known as they walked out onto the ice bridge that disaster lurked.

One of Niagara's most incredible attractions, the ice bridge is a natural phenomenon that residents and tourists alike marveled at. On the day of the Stantons' visit, hundreds of people were on hand to view the spectacle. Some were locals, but many—like Eldridge and Clara—had come from Toronto aboard special excursion trains.

For the ice bridge to form, it is dependent upon specific climatic conditions that usually appear in January and last until mid-February. The bridge is created when a mixture of ice and slush flows down from Lake Erie, drops over the falls and is forced up alongside the shores. The river jams with more and more ice and slush, gradually increasing in size and density, the whole mass beginning to heave and hump from the continuous pressure. Eventually, the mass builds up to such an extent that the river becomes encased in a thick layer of ice, creating a "bridge" that reaches across the Niagara River from shore to shore. In places almost 60 feet thick, the ice bridge is strong enough to easily support the weight of hundreds of people.

Throughout the 19th century, local residents ventured out onto the ice to view the falls in a whole new light, but word spread, and by the early 1880s the ice bridge became a popular winter playground, an attraction that lured thousands every year from across the United States and Canada. Businessmen, eager to exploit the opportunity, even set up concession shanties on the ice, where drinks—including whiskey—could be purchased, to warm the soul on cold bitter days; also available were hot dogs for the kids and souvenirs. Tourists could even have a tintype picture taken of themselves on the ice bridge.

As a tourist attraction, the ice bridge was a place of excitement and revelry. But it also masked a hidden danger that could reveal itself at any moment. On the day that Eldridge and Clara Stanton strolled out onto the frozen river, few could have imagined that a terrible tragedy lay in store.

As the Stantons walked along the ice bridge and chatted about their future with excitement dancing

The Ice Mountain, Niagara Falls.

Most winters, an ice bridge spanning the Niagara River forms below the falls. In the early 20th century, it was a popular pastime to stroll out onto the ice, purchase hot dogs from vendors and pose for photos with the ice-draped falls as a backdrop.

~·❀·~

in their eyes, they didn't notice the crowds begin to die down as noon approached and people headed indoors to get warm and have some lunch. By noon, only about 25 people were on the ice. The Stantons were enjoying their morning and, oblivious to the biting cold, continued to walk farther out onto the frozen sheet.

Eldridge and Clara noticed two young fellows walking in front of them. Husband and wife looked at each other as if thinking the same thing; they were ready for children and looking forward to that special day when they would be parents.

Despite their youthfulness, the two 17-year-old boys, Ignatius Roth and Burell Hecock, would prove to be more courageous than they looked. Being lifelong friends, they did everything together and always had, and the ice bridge seemed on this cold winter day to be just another place for these Cleveland natives to explore together. Also on the ice that day was William "Red" Hill Sr., a well-known river man from Niagara Falls, Ontario, who later rose to fame for saving the crew of the scow stranded above the falls.

Mother Nature often strikes without warning, her vengeance coming with a suddenness and ferocity that leaves humans with no defense. Certainly, no one on the ice that day had any hint of impending danger, at least not until a loud and horrible cracking sound suddenly echoed through the gorge. The ice began to shake underfoot, becoming a tremor that made everyone on the ice bridge struggle to keep their footing. Moments later, another rumble erupted, followed by the shriek of ice buckling. Cracks appeared in the ice, tearing jagged fingers across the frozen sheet. The ice bridge was breaking up!

Red Hill reacted quickly. He raced for shore and cried out to the others on the ice to run for their lives to safety. He reached the Canadian shore, as did many others. Some made it to the American side. All were thought to have reached safety until four figures were seen standing on the rapidly disintegrating ice bridge: Eldridge, Clara, Ignatius Roth and Burell Hecock.

They all hesitated, not sure which way to go. In places, cracks had now become channels several feet wide, threatening to cut them off if they didn't react immediately. Large ice floes had already broken free to be swept downriver, and it was just a matter of time before the ice bridge shattered completely. The two boys made a dash for the Canadian shore, while the Stantons went in the opposite direction, only to find their escape blocked by a chasm too wide to jump. The ice was breaking up into floes all around them. They were in serious trouble.

Red Hill risked his own life by rushing back onto the ice, where he hoped the Stantons could hear him, telling them to head for the Canadian side. With the experienced river man guiding them around hazards and yelling words of encouragement, the couple made it to within 50 feet of the river bank, when they suddenly encountered another wide, slush-filled channel. Ignatius and Burell joined the couple, but their escape was also blocked by wide gaps filled with angry, freezing water. It seemed hopeless for all of them.

Paralyzed with fear, Eldridge and Clara couldn't bring themselves to go on, even though Hill promised them the gap could be crossed. Instead, the couple turned back, searching for another avenue of escape. With the ice bridge crumbling faster by the moment, Hill had no choice but to flee for his safety and leave them behind as he once again scrambled to shore.

By now, the large ice floe that carried the marooned foursome was floating toward danger. The Stantons were exhausted from the exertion and tension, and Clara collapsed as Ignatius and Burell raced ahead, hoping to find a spot where they might leap onto another floe and then to safety. Unable to rise, Clara begged her husband to go on without her, but Eldridge refused to abandon her. Instead, he shouted to the two youths for help as he struggled to lift his wife to her feet.

The two boys looked back, but only Burell Hecock returned to help. He left his lifelong buddy and selflessly risked his fate to assist strangers in danger. Ignatius Roth, meanwhile, left the others behind and ran for his life. He managed to get close to the Canadian shore, where Red Hill, who was running along the river bank, shouted instructions. Roth did as he was told, jumping over openings where and when he was directed and struggling over the hummocks of ice. When the lad was close enough, Hill threw him a rope and pulled him ashore, slightly more than a mile below the Horseshoe Falls. Ignatius Roth did not die that day; he had cheated death.

Meanwhile, the ice floe carrying the three remaining helpless victims was racing ever faster down the river and soon would reach the Whirlpool Rapids, known as one of the most violent stretches of white water in the world. Their last chance at rescue were the ropes that police and firefighters lowered from the Cantilever Bridge and the adjacent Whirlpool Rapids Bridge. It was a slender chance, but it was all they had.

Just before reaching the bridge, the ice floe broke in two, separating the Stantons from young Hecock. Hecock was the first to reach one of the dangling ropes. Cold and near frozen, he grabbed hold of the rope with numbed hands and hung on for dear life, as rescuers tried to pull him up. The young man tried to climb hand over hand, but with frozen fingers and exhaustion setting in, he found it difficult to hang on.

Eldridge and Clara Stanton, and Burell Hecock, went to their deaths when the ice bridge below the falls suddenly broke up. The three figures can just be seen on the ice floes near the center of the photo.

Hecock's grip began to slip. He was losing sensation in his hands. Desperately, he tried to get his legs around the rope, and when this failed, he made a heart-wrenching attempt to hang on with his teeth. Unfortunately, the rope kept spinning, making it even more difficult to hang on. He was 40 feet in the air, one-third of the way to safety, but his strength was failing rapidly. Finally, as if knowing it was hopeless, and exhausted by the fight, Hecock let his head fall back and let go of his grip. The rescuers on the bridge above watched with a mixture of sadness and horror as he plummeted toward the frigid waters.

The young man who turned back to help strangers in danger, who did not even think of his own safety, fell to his watery death in the icy cold abyss below.

Now the ice floe carrying the Stantons reached the Cantilever Bridge. Eldridge grabbed hold of a rope with hands numbed by the intense cold. He made no attempt to save himself; Eldridge thought only of the woman he dearly loved. He would gladly have given his life to save hers. He desperately struggled to get the rope around Clara's waist before they were swept past the bridge, but with the ice moving so quickly and his reflexes slowed by the cold, it proved impossible. The rope slid from his grip before he had a chance to tie it around his wife.

A second attempt at rescue was made from the Whirlpool Rapids Bridge, again without success.

There was no hope for the Stantons now, and they knew it. With his breath blowing in frosty vapors, Eldridge consoled his wife and held her close. Perhaps, with all hope of rescue gone, they welcomed death, so long as they could meet it together.

An eyewitness described the final moments of the unfolding drama: "He raised the woman to her feet, kissed her and clasped her in his arms. The woman then sank to her knees. The man knelt beside her; his arms clasped close about her. So they went to their death. The ice held intact until it struck the great wave. There it shattered; there the gallant man and the woman at his side disappeared from view."

News of the deaths was startling enough to make the front pages of the *New York Times,* and in the aftermath, people tried to come to terms with the catastrophe. A monument to young hero Burell Hecock was raised in Queen Victoria Park, keeping alive the memory of a boy whose life was cut short by his selflessness. The Canadian and American governments agreed they could not, in good conscience, allow the practice of venturing out onto the ice bridge to continue. Thereafter, no one was permitted to venture onto the ice bridge.

Prior to 1912, no one could have imagined that a day spent exploring the beautiful ice bridge at Niagara Falls, as people had done for decades, would have turned into such a horrible tragedy. And yet, a romantic stroll on the ice had ended any dreams Eldridge and Clara Stanton had for their future together, snuffing out lives full of promise.

Although their bodies were never found, and their time on Earth was tragically cut short, one hopes that the love they had for each other carried them to eternal peace together.

Scow Daring River Rescue

James Harris is trapped. He and Gustave Lofberg are prisoners of the Niagara River, stranded on a barge amid the thundering rapids just above the falls. The barge is grounded on rocks but is being lashed by waves that could at any moment free it and send Harris and Lofberg to a watery grave. The men feel helpless and terrified. Without warning, their worst fear becomes reality. One too many waves hits the barge, finally prying it from the rocks' grip. The craft is pulled relentlessly down the Niagara River. The roar of the falls is deafening and grows louder with each passing moment. Harris watches with a combination of horror and fascination as the drop rapidly approaches. Then the barge slides over the falls and out from beneath his feet. He feels a weightlessness as he plummets into the mist below....

And then Harris wakes in a cold sweat. It is the middle of the night, and he is having the same haunting dream that visits him nightly, over and over. In his nightmares, he relives the frightening events of that day back in August 1918. The day he and Lofberg almost died. They had escaped death that day, but what Harris couldn't escape, what fueled his nightmares, was the realization that he had nearly met that fate.

The afternoon of August 6, 1918, was particularly hot and muggy. Harris would remember the stifling heat and breath-stealing humidity until the day he died. He and Gustave Lofberg, who at 51 was two years his junior, were crewing a scow in the Upper Niagara River, near Buffalo. Both men were employees of the Great Lakes Dredge and Dock Company, and it was their job to deepen the intake canal for the Niagara Falls Power Company.

Harris and Lofberg felt secure aboard the scow, a sturdy, flat-bottomed barge measuring 80 feet long and 30 feet wide. It wasn't an attractive vessel, but it was built strong and was well-suited to its work. One of the scow's most interesting features were the six hoppers in its hull, which carried the silt dredged from the river bottom. The hoppers had large doors in the bottom, so the silt could be dumped when required. To stay afloat when the hopper doors were open, the scow was designed with air-tight compartments. In short, the vessel was built to be almost unsinkable.

At 3:00 PM, the tug *Hassayampa* arrived to tow in the scow and take her back to shore. Harris and Lofberg smiled contentedly; their shift was over. Another day, another dollar. They settled back to enjoy the ride home. A few minutes later, however, the two men heard a loud snapping sound. Suddenly alert, they stood up and, to their horror, saw that the tow cable had snapped. The scow was now free and at the mercy of the Niagara River. The scow was swept down the river by the raging current, heading toward the white-capped rapids above the Horseshoe Falls. The *Hassayampa* and two other tugs that happened to be on the river gave chase, but they couldn't keep pace with the out-of-control barge.

Harris and Lofberg realized there would be no rescue; their survival lay in their own hands. Working frantically to bring the scow to a stop before it reached the thunderous waterfall, they tried every desperate measure they could imagine. First, they threw an anchor overboard, but in the rocky bottom it found no hold, and the scow continued unabated. Next, they opened the doors on the scow, hoping they would become lodged on some rock and stop or slow the scow's headway. Still, the scow continued its relentless advance downriver.

Finally, now shaking with terror, the two crewmen opened the sea-cocks to the air-tight compartments to allow the scow to sink. It started to but not fast enough, and time was rapidly running out. The situation appeared hopeless. Only a few thousand feet lay between them and the precipice. The men had perhaps a few minutes left to live. They prayed and thought of their loved ones. They regretted things not said and deeds left undone.

Harris and Lofberg could hear the falls approaching, and it was the sound of 100 steam locomotives rushing toward them. Then, almost miraculously, the half-forgotten anchor snagged and held fast. The scow ground to a sudden halt on Rock Shoal and, as water poured through the opened doors, settled on the bottom of the river. Only 800 feet away, the falls roared ominously, as if angered to have been deprived of its victims. The Toronto Electrical Development Powerhouse and the Canadian shore was a similar distance away, but with the deadly rapids between, it might as well have been 100 miles.

News of the men's plight spread rapidly, and soon, members of the Niagara Falls Fire Department arrived on scene. Locals began to congregate along the shores, numbering first in the dozens and later the hundreds. The unfolding drama kept them captivated, their collective breaths held. The powerhouse had been guarded against sabotage since the outbreak of World War I four years earlier, so even soldiers from the army were on hand. But nobody had the slightest idea what to do to help the stranded sailors. Nothing like this had ever happened before.

The fire department tried to use a grappling gun to shoot a lifeline out from the roof of the powerhouse, but it fell short by about 500 feet. Next they tried to attach safety lines to a wooden raft and float it out to the stricken craft from upriver. With the unpredictable current of the Niagara River, the odds of the raft passing within reach of the scow were remote. But they had to try something. Predictably enough, the attempt failed. Shortly after 4:00 PM, Ross Coddington, the superintendent of construction of the Hydraulic Power Company, phoned the United States Coast Guard lifeboat station at Fort Niagara, New York. If anyone had the specialized training and equipment for such a high-risk maritime rescue, he reasoned, it would be the Coast Guard.

Forty-five minutes later, the Coast Guard arrived on the scene with a heavier grappling gun than that possessed by the Niagara Falls Fire Department and Breeches Buoy rescue equipment (a canvas sling suspended from a pulley). They raced to set up their gear, fearing that the anchor would lose its grip at any moment. The line was fired. Bull's eye! It landed directly on board the scow. But Harris and Lofberg were not safe yet. The line wasn't strong enough to support their weight. For that, a much thicker rope was needed. Lofberg had been a saltwater sailor and knew a great deal about handling ships and their rigging. Under his supervision, he and Harris set up a winch from the scow's door-closing apparatus and used it to drag a heavier rope out to them through the raging waters.

At first, they made little headway. The rope sagged into the river, where the angry current took hold of it. The two stranded men fought against the fury of Mother Nature, arms and backs on fire as they strained to drag the rope toward them.

Coast Guard Captain Nelson realized the two men had little chance of success unless something was done to help. He recruited the milling onlookers to assist, ordering them to help pull the thick rope taut, so that its length didn't drag through the river. With less resistance, Harris and Lofberg began to make greater progress, though it was still painfully slow, the rope only moving three inches closer per turn of the improvised winch.

It wasn't until 2:00 AM that the line was finally secured aboard the scow, while the shore end was tied fast to the street car tracks that ran along the river bank. The two crewmen collapsed into exhausted heaps on board, drained from the terror and exertion of the day. But they were confident that their rescue was near at hand.

But a snag appeared in the plan, literally, as it turned out. When the Breeches Buoy was set up, the lines quickly fouled. Until they could be freed, the stranded men weren't going anywhere. To free them, someone had to go out to the ropes above the torturous water and untangle them by hand. Captain Nelson looked into the eyes of his men, the firefighters, even the onlookers. He saw in none of them a willingness to make the risky attempt, and he wasn't about to order anyone to do it. He wouldn't have someone's death on his hands. But then the crowds parted, and a volunteer stepped forward: William "Red" Hill, a famous Niagara river man who had already done more than his share of rescuing on the river that he both loved and feared. Hill had just returned from fighting in France, where he had been wounded and gassed, but despite his weakened condition, he was eager to offer his services. He volunteered to go out and untangle the lines.

Hill made his way out to the ropes and painstakingly worked to clear them. His efforts, however, were handicapped by darkness and by his own fatigue from the exertion. Even when he was successful in clearing one knot, Hill found to his dismay that the line was tangled again farther out. He realized at this point that the rescue effort would have to be put off until daylight. His heart went out to the men trapped aboard the scow, but it was simply too difficult and too dangerous to continue in the darkness.

The men on board spent a fearful, sleepless night. The temperature remained stiflingly hot, and they were exhausted and hungry, convinced with every groan of the hull that the scow was about to break loose and go over the falls. Rescuers ashore had the same concerns, so they requested that all five hydroelectric plants on the Niagara River operate at full capacity so as to use as much water as possible. It was reasoned that with lower water levels, the scow had less chance of being dislodged.

At daylight, Hill went back out to clear the tangled rope. This time he was successful and could get close enough to the scow to shout instructions.

By 9:00 AM, the rescue buoy was sent out. Harris, the worse off of the two crewmen, blue-lipped and at the point of collapse from exhaustion, got in first. The people onshore watched aghast as the weakened man almost slipped into the roiling waves below, but he managed to hold on and reach safety. Lofberg came next, but after the drama of Harris' rescue, his was somewhat anticlimactic. Still relatively strong, he was easily pulled to shore, landing on the roof of the powerhouse at 10:24 AM.

As soon as they reached shore, Harris and Lofberg were mobbed by relieved rescuers, a throng of concerned onlookers and reporters eager to tell the men's story. Bundled in blankets, the two men were led to the nearby Cataract House hotel, where they soaked in hot baths, ate a hearty breakfast then tumbled into warm beds for a sound sleep. Incredibly, despite being trapped aboard the scow and in the elements for 28 hours, neither had suffered serious illness or injury. A doctor examined them both and noted that, though fatigued, the men were in good health. The two men reported back to work the following day.

Lofberg, in fact, seemed to take pride in his newfound fame. He reveled in the telling of his near-death experience and capitalized on it by speaking at local theaters before rapt crowds. His moment in the spotlight was short-lived, however, and he went back to sea. His eventual fate is something of a mystery, but one report suggests he died in World

War II, when a German submarine sunk the ship he was serving on. Harris, for his part, had no interest in talking about the experience. The episode had scarred him for life, and he became deathly afraid of the Niagara River. He quit his job for one ashore, refused to go anywhere near the river and was traumatized by nightmares until his death in 1939.

No serious attempt was made to salvage the scow, even though it was valued at $60,000. Rewards were offered for its recovery, but no one had any idea how to go about doing so. It remained grounded in the middle of the river and over time

The rusting hulk of a barge rests dangerously near the lip of the falls, run aground on rocks and unmoving for decades. The tempestuous waters and proximity to the falls makes it easy to appreciate the difficulties involved in rescuing the barge's trapped crewmen.

became something of a local landmark. It's still there today. Trees grow out of its hold, having taken root in some of the dredge soil remaining in the scow. The hull is rusted red, and some of the deck and side plates have disappeared due to the pounding of the elements. But the scow shows no sign of breaking up anytime soon.

Ninety years later, the scow serves as a point of interest for millions of tourists every year and a reminder of one of Niagara River's greatest rescues.

Honeymoon Bridge Collapse

The massive bridge threatened to collapse into the Niagara gorge below. Metal girders supporting the span were heaving, and it was obvious it would soon break apart, like river ice at the spring thaw. Suddenly, the bridge buckled violently, as if in protest.

Moments before, sneaking past the guards and onto the crippled structure had seemed like a harmless adventure for two young boys, Douglas and Wesley Styles, aged 12 and 13. But as the bridge swayed underfoot and the metal groaned threateningly, the two looked at one another aghast, eyes wide in terror. What minutes before had been mischievous fun now seemed like a terrible and perhaps fatal mistake.

The metal beneath them shivered and writhed again. The young boys ran for the safety of shore, but the span swayed violently, and they almost lost their footing. Terrified, the boys bolted for safety, with the trembling bridge threatening to trip them with every step. They reached the shore just as the metal bowed and buckled. And they kept running.

With a thundering groan, a rumbling roar that echoed the length of the gorge, Niagara's Honeymoon Bridge fell, collapsing onto the icy surface of the river far below.

Douglas and Wesley shivered where they stood, then sat down abruptly. They were silent; the catastrophe they had been a part of, the nearness of their death, bore down on them like a crushing weight. When Douglas finally broke the silence, only one thing emerged from his quivering lips: "I hope Mom doesn't find out about this."

Mom did find out. All of Niagara found out. Most of North America found out. The collapse of the Honeymoon Bridge on January 27, 1938, captivated millions on both sides of the border, and journalists, anxious for additional drama to sell the story, focused on the experiences of the Styles boys. It was a thrilling sideline to what was already a thoroughly captivating story.

The Honeymoon Bridge, so-called because so many newlyweds crossed from the United States on their way to romantic honeymoons in Niagara Falls, Ontario, was built 40 years earlier in 1898. When completed on June 30 of that year, the bridge, which spanned the Niagara River gorge, was officially named the Upper Steel Arch Bridge, or Fallsview Bridge.

But the structure was always more than just a collection of wood and steel. It was an example of modern engineering and ingenuity, a construction marvel for its day. Furthermore, because Canada and the United States had jointly built the bridge, it represented solidarity and peace between the two neighbors, as if the span linked two hands in friendship. Many people viewing it felt a surge of pride and awe at what the two nations could accomplish together.

For exactly four decades, the Honeymoon Bridge dominated the profile of the Niagara River gorge looking downstream from the falls. Then, in late January 1938, this proud pinnacle of engineering was suddenly brought crashing down by the forces of nature.

Starting on January 25, an enormous ice jam developed in the Niagara River gorge immediately below the falls. This wasn't altogether unusual. Every winter, for a period of few weeks, an ice bridge forms here, made mostly from ice floes that come down from Lake Erie, break up into smaller pieces in the upper rapids, plunge over the falls and then mass together in the lower river from shore to shore. But what was unusual this year was the sheer amount of ice. Normally, the ice bridge forms just at the base of the falls, but in late January 1938 the heaving ice was so extensive that it spread a mile or more downstream. In the process, the two *Maid of the Mist* boats were pushed off their winter berths on shore and their docks were destroyed.

The volume of ice was exceptional but not immediately worrying. Those living along the river had long grown accustomed to unusual weather. But by the early hours of January 26, people started to grow alarmed as ice began to pile up around the pillars of the Honeymoon Bridge in quantities never seen before, putting immense strain on the steel supports. Maintenance crews were summoned to the scene in a desperate attempt to save the structure. They climbed down into the gorge and frantically cleared ice away from the pillars. Sweat froze to their bodies as they raced with shovels and picks to keep ahead of the rising ice. Within a few hours it became apparent that they were fighting a losing battle; the ice was simply accumulating faster than they could remove it.

Meanwhile, engineers inspecting the structure made a startling discovery: several of the support girders were beginning to buckle under the immense strain. At 9:15 AM, the decision was made to close the bridge and suspend ice-clearing efforts. The Honeymoon Bridge was left to her fate.

By the next morning, the ice jam stretched from the river bottom to a height of 150 feet, creating a virtual dam. Popping rivets could be heard as the bridge groaned under the strain, and everyone on shore knew that it was just a matter of time before the doomed bridge gave up the struggle and collapsed. As word of her imminent demise spread, thousands of curious spectators, newspaper reporters and photographers were drawn to the scene, braving the cold to watch the death of a landmark. Police set up a barrier on both sides of the bridge, preventing people from getting too close. But security wasn't tight enough to stop two adventurous boys from slipping past and onto the bridge.

When asked later why they did it, Douglas and Wesley Styles answered that they had simply wanted to get a better point of view from which to take pictures of the spectacular ice formations in the gorge below. The best spot, they decided, was from the bridge itself. The structure still seemed safe enough, and besides, they really wouldn't be on it for very long. What was the harm?

The police represented a problem, so the boys had to be fast and quiet to slip past them. They waited until the nearest officer turned his back, and then, hunched over to make themselves small, they slowly made their through the barrier and toward the doomed bridge. Once they were clear, the boys ran. It was easier than they had imagined it would be, and, as they suspected, the bridge seemed sound enough. Douglas and Wesley made their way farther out over the river, looking for just the right shot.

The boys were a considerable distance from shore when they finally stopped to take that once-in-a-lifetime picture they were looking for. One of the boys was just steadying the camera to snap the shot when the bridge suddenly shook. Rivets popped like gunshots, metal groaned and the ground shifted underfoot. The bridge trembled as the moving ice, some 60 feet in height, literally pushed it off its footings on the American side. The Honeymoon Bridge had only minutes left, and so, too, did the boys, unless they acted quickly. They ran for their lives, faster than they thought themselves capable of, fear and adrenaline driving their legs to greater speed. The bridge behind them, starting from the center, began to collapse, sections falling away at their heels. Incredibly, they reached

Even the best engineered structures can be brought down by the forces of nature, as the sudden collapse of the Honeymoon Bridge spanning the Niagara River aptly demonstrated.

safety just as the historic structure fell. From the time the bridge was pushed off its footings to the moment of its collapse took no more than 10 seconds. The time was 4:20 PM.

Hearts pounding, oblivious to the mayhem of excited onlookers around them, the boys peered over the edge of the gorge. The bridge lay in a crumpled heap on the frozen river, broken into four main sections. What had just days before been an engineering marvel was now little more than a mass of warped steel and wood. If they had been a mere second slower, the Styles boys realized, they too would be lying broken on the ice below. It was a frightening thought. Worse was the thought of what punishment lay in store for them once mom found out how foolish they had been.

Newspapers across Canada and the United States flashed the story of the bridge's demise on front pages. The *Niagara Falls Review* recorded the death of the bridge in dramatic fashion:

> *With startling suddenness, and what sounded like a weary groan, the mighty structure sagged and fell into the gorge. There was not a great deal of noise as the 2600 tons of steel and 300 tons of wood, which comprised the framework and floor of the bridge, sank to rest, and onlookers scarcely believed their eyes as they saw the destruction of the once proud span which now lies in the shape of a great twisted "W" on the ice bridge.*

The following Sunday, Niagara Falls experienced one of the busiest days in its history, as thousands came from as far away as Toronto and even New York City to view the remains of the shattered and broken bridge. Some simply couldn't believe that the landmark was gone, destroyed by ice. Crowds of curious onlookers lined the shores, and brave individuals ventured out onto the ice to collect souvenirs. Enterprising souls even sold remnants of the Honeymoon Bridge: rivets, twisted metal and slivers of wood.

Engineers were worried that the mass would cause an obstruction in the river, and it was deemed prudent to break it up into smaller pieces. Rather than cut it up, a painstaking process, on February 5, dynamite was used to break the wreckage into six pieces. The plan was practical but not well thought out; the blast shattered windows throughout Niagara Falls, causing about $10,000 worth of damage. Clearly, too many explosives were used, but it sure made for an exciting spectacle for the viewers lining the shores.

The remains of the Honeymoon Bridge lay on the ice until the spring thaw. On April 12, the ice bridge began to break up, and most of the bridge debris slipped from sight under the water where it had fallen. A section 250 feet in length was the sole survivor; it floated downriver on a large ice floe. At 4:00 PM, amid loud cracking noises as the ice underneath broke up, the twisted metal slid beneath the waves about a mile downriver from the falls, erasing all remnants of the once-spectacular Honeymoon Bridge.

Planning began almost immediately for a new bridge to link Niagara Falls, Ontario, with Niagara Falls, New York, though it was decided to build it 500 feet farther downriver. On June 7, 1939, King George VI and Queen Elizabeth, parents of the current ruling monarch, Elizabeth II, cut the ribbon on this site during a brief ceremony. Ground was officially broken for the construction of what became the Rainbow Bridge on May 4, 1940. When completed, at a cost of $3.76 million, the bridge's 950-foot steel arch was the longest hingeless arch in the world.

Thousands of honeymooners continue to come to Niagara Falls annually via this new bridge, blissfully unaware of the drama that took place there years before. They pass over it with hopes of making memories that will last a lifetime. But the collapse of the earlier Honeymoon Bridge left its share of other memories, not all of them pleasant. For two young boys, it left lifelong memories of a day when they nearly went down in history along with the bridge.

CHAPTER SIX

Tourism Comes to Niagara

WHEN IT COMES TO Niagara, everyone thinks first of the falls, without a doubt the primary reason tourists visit the region. And it's been that way since tourism first came to Niagara in the early 19th century.

As early as 1820, wealthy Americans from the South, attempting to escape the stifling heat and humidity of the Carolinas and Georgia, considered a pilgrimage to Niagara Falls to be the high point of what came to be known as the "Fashionable Tour." Over a period of several months, they visited all the cultural and natural highlights of the temperate American northeast, including New York City and Boston, but Niagara Falls was the one sight no self-respecting aristocrat would ever miss.

For these people of means, Niagara represented an opportunity to live for a few days or weeks in a setting of perfect beauty, to experience something that gave them profound pleasure and, perhaps most importantly, also asserted their membership among the cultural elite.

From the 1820s, hotelkeepers and entrepreneurs in Niagara began to shape the land surrounding the falls with these aristocratic tourists in mind. Visitors enjoyed well-appointed hotels, landscaped paths and gardens, carriages offering tranquil rides along the river, hawkers selling food and wares and staircases that descended to the bottom of the gorge below the falls. It was all very exciting but also very expensive and exclusive, the sole domain of the wealthy and the privileged.

The average folk knew that Niagara was not for them, and only housemaids, ferrymen, guides and others who served the tourist trade lived at the falls. The locals may have resented this intrusion, but they also realized that they were enriched by the annual invasion of the upper classes, who paid well for food and rented horses and provided seasonal work.

Within a few decades, things began to slowly change. Although the falls was the exclusive domain of the wealthy in the summer, hotelkeepers created off-season festivals for local crowds, staged in autumn, after the fashionable visitors had returned home for the year. It wasn't that entrepreneurs were worried about social equality or were motivated by some moral desire to open up the falls to the common man. Their sole concern was making a buck; extending the season and encouraging less-affluent visitors meant more money could be made.

Many of the attractions associated with Niagara today—the thrill ride of the Spanish Aero Car that crosses over the whirlpool suspended on cables, the exhilaration of the Journey Behind the Falls, the *Maid of the Mist* tour boat that ventures daringly close to the thundering wall of water and even the stunningly beautiful floral gardens of Queen Victoria Park—emerged more than a century ago, during the early years of tourism in Niagara.

Thankfully, at the same time, most of the less-savory attempts at profiteering have been eliminated. It's hard to imagine anyone would miss the houses of ill-repute that proliferated in the 1860s, the "spectacle" of sending boats laden with animals over the falls or even the thrilling but extremely dangerous practice of venturing onto the ice-encrusted river within the gorge.

Visitors of today will be pleasantly surprised by the diversity of the region. The falls remain the main attraction, but there is much more to see and do. What few visitors recognize are the many fascinating stories centered on the development of tourism in Niagara driven by the greed in attempts to profit by the natural wonder.

The Pavilion, Niagara's First Grand Hotel

In the Niagara Falls of today, one can find many hotels offering luxury accommodations, fine hospitality and beautiful views overlooking the rapids and falls. Each has its own distinct charms, its own merit, something unique to provide guests. But all have one thing in common: they are spiritual descendants of the Pavilion Hotel, the first luxury tourist hotel in Niagara Falls. For more than a decade, it was the place to be and be seen.

The Pavilion Hotel was the brainchild of William Forsyth, one of Niagara's earliest entrepreneurs in the tourism industry but also a shameless and aggressive opportunist with a disreputable past. Born in the United States in 1774, he developed a somewhat shady reputation early on. In 1799, he was charged with a felony but acquitted. A few years later, he was found guilty of another unspecified crime and jailed. Forsyth escaped from prison and made a desperate attempt at flight but was apprehended before he could reach the safety of the United States, and he was dragged back to his cell, shackled but still defiant.

During the War of 1812, Forsyth, described as a "small wiry man, weighing barely 150 pounds," fought with the British as part of the 2nd Lincoln Militia. Sometimes he served valiantly but often more dubiously. His commanding officer, Thomas Clark, suggested he was not much liked by his fellow soldiers, who described him as "a man of uncouth behavior" and indicated that he was prone to cowardice and deceit.

In the post-war period, Forsyth found a new opportunity to exploit. Since 1815, Niagara Falls has attracted wealthy world travelers—Americans, predominantly—intent on seeing the renowned natural wonder in person. Niagara Falls, once so remote, was now easily accessible to those with money. The upper classes rested comfortably in 80-foot, horse-drawn canal boats, coasting along at a leisurely four miles per hour. Upon reaching Buffalo, carriages and ferries were waiting to take them to their ultimate destination at the falls. However, there was little to encourage well-heeled visitors to dally—no tourist hotel to wrap them in the luxury they expected.

Forsyth envisioned he could remedy that and profit handsomely by it. His plan began in 1817, when he purchased Wilson's Tavern, a Niagara inn built in 1797, which he quickly renamed the Niagara Hotel. In 1821, Forsyth purchased more than 100 acres surrounding the hotel, and a year later, he tore down the aging structure and in its place built the luxurious Pavilion Hotel.

The building, which was located just north of where the Minolta Tower now stands, was three stories high, of white clapboard construction that boasted covered verandahs overlooking the falls and rapids. Horatio Parson's guidebook of 1836 noted, "the Pavilion has an imposing appearance, and from the observatory on its roof visitors have an extensive view of the surrounding country."

Because it catered to the society's elite, the Pavilion included a well-stocked library, a piano, billiard tables and accommodations for "noblemen and gentlemen of the highest rank with their families." Forsyth made sure to stock the hotel with "viands from every land" as well as "the best flavoured and most costly wines and liquors."

The Pavilion was by far the largest and most famous hotel in Niagara at the time, accommodating as many as 150 guests in style, many of whom remained for weeks or even months at a time. Among the prominent guests were two Governors General of British North America, the Duke of Richmond and Lord Dalhousie; writer Frances Trollope; and poet Lydia Sigourney, who called the falls "beautiful and glorious."

Adam Fergusson, a wealthy Scottish traveler, stayed at the Pavilion in 1831. Upon arriving, he noted, "a splendid and extensive establishment." If his writings are an indication, Fergusson spent most of his time lounging in the hotel's notably well-stocked bar. "I scarce recollect of anything more welcome than a beverage with which my companion regaled me at Forsyth's, under some name, but which consisted of a bottle of good brown stout turned into a quart of iced water, with a sufficient quantity of ginger, cinnamon and sugar," he penned. "Truly it was a prescription worthy of being filled."

Fergusson and his seemingly unquenchable appetite for alcohol aside, the main attraction for any stay at the Pavilion was the view of the falls. And, although the hotel's rooftop view was "unequalled for grandeur and diversity," Forsyth knew visitors wanted to see the falls up close. It was as if the raging waters called out to them; the combination of overwhelming power and beauty was impossible to resist. Forsyth catered to this impulse by clearing a path from the Pavilion down to the lip of the falls but ensured that trees and shrubbery remained to obstruct the view, so that the full impact of the spectacle burst suddenly upon the senses at the end, and not before. It was brilliant showmanship, and visitors loved it.

Guests also loved the spiral staircase Forsyth built that descended to the base of the falls. The stairs' wooden siding guarded against vertigo and a premature view of the falls that might spoil the finale. At the entrance, guests paid a toll, signed a guest book and then passed down the stairs and through a guide's shack, emerging only a few feet from the violence at the base of the falls. If they so chose, they could also don water-resistant clothing and walk behind the curtain of water, an adventure that thousands eagerly experienced.

As a result of the hotel's grandeur, as well as the carefully crafted Niagara experience that Forsyth provided guests, the Pavilion was a success from the moment its doors opened in 1822. It was something to behold, a destination in itself, and during its first summer—and for every summer for 10 years thereafter—it was fully booked almost every night. To keep up with demand, an ambitious expansion that included two new wings was undertaken in 1826. In addition, Forsyth acquired stakes in a stage coach line and ferry service that brought patrons to Niagara in general and his hotel specifically.

William Forsyth was undeniably the leading figure when it came to selling the falls as a tourist attraction. But he wasn't the only one, and as the decade wore on, competition from other hotels became fiercer. That didn't sit well with Forsyth. The falls was big enough to share, but that wasn't his style. Forsyth didn't want just a piece of Niagara Falls, he wanted the whole thing and would go to just about any lengths, stoop to any depths, to get it. When rival hotelier John Brown built a plank road from his Ontario House hotel to the falls, Forsyth promptly ripped it up. When Thomas Clark and Samuel Street acquired ferry rights on the river, Forsyth harassed and sabotaged the operation so aggressively it couldn't operate. And when Ontario House burned to the ground under mysterious circumstances in 1826, many in town pointed the finger at Forsyth as the likely culprit. The accused made little attempt to dissuade this opinion; when asked about the fire, he simply smiled knowingly but remained silent.

Finally, however, perhaps having grown flush with his success and the ease with which he thumbed his nose at the law, Forsyth pushed his luck too far, and it cost him dearly. In 1827, he built a plank fence around the Pavilion and down to the banks of the Niagara, enclosing part of the shoreline and laying claim to it as his own. But this wasn't just any stretch of river; enclosed within Forsyth's self-proclaimed domain was Niagara's ultimate prize, Table Rock.

Table Rock was a huge platform of rock, several acres in size, that once hung more than 50 feet over the gorge just above the lip of the falls. From the edge, sightseers were no more than five feet from the raging waters below, so close that they could almost dip their toes into the waters. The bravest people crept to the edge nearest the falls and peered out over the wondrous vista. Over the years, as the rock beneath it eroded and crumbled, vast slabs of it tumbled away until, bit by bit, Table Rock disappeared. But that wasn't until much later. In the 1820s, Table Rock was the favored spot from which to view the falls. If one could take possession of Table Rock, as Forsyth realized, he could monopolize tourism at Niagara Falls.

Once the opportunistic entrepreneur put up his fence, the only way to enjoy that favored viewpoint was through his hotel and only after paying a fee. The other hotelkeepers were enraged. Forsyth was trying to grab the Niagara experience for himself. The public was equally enraged. The average person couldn't afford to pay admission. Desperate letters were written to the government, after which the lieutenant-governor forcefully reminded Forsyth that a strip of land along the edge of the river 66 feet deep was reserved for the Crown and was not in actuality part of his property. In other words, the fence was illegal, and the falls was a public treasure to be enjoyed by all.

Soldiers were sent to tear the fence down, in the process trampling Forsyth's crops and destroying his blacksmith shop. Forsyth was undeterred; he simply rebuilt the fence and awaited a response. Perhaps he thought the government wouldn't dispatch soldiers a second time for what was really a minor issue better settled in the courts. If so, he underestimated the will of the government. Soldiers were sent in a second time, and once again they ripped down the offending fence.

Enraged by this gross misuse of government power, and still confident that he was in the right, Forsyth launched a costly civil suit against the government. He lost. He lost again when Brown sued him for tearing up his road. And Forsyth lost a third time when Clark and Street sued him for ruining their ferry service.

The stubborn hotelier refused to give up, even though he had little chance of success against his rivals. Forsyth didn't have the political connections his opponents enjoyed. Thomas Clark was a miller and merchant, a powerful member of the community and a former member of the Legislative Council who had the ear of the lieutenant-governor. Samuel Street was equally rich and powerful, a miller who was also a moneylender.

The fact that he had other prominent people in his debt gave him an edge that Forsyth couldn't command.

Forsyth must have known the cards were stacked against him, and yet he refused to fold. In fact, he upped the ante by attempting to counter-sue his opponents twice. Both were expensive and frustrating failures as well. In the end, after five years and a fortune spent in court, Forsyth was a beaten and despondent man.

In 1833, William Forsyth finally admitted defeat. He sold the hotel to his rivals, Street and Clark. The wounds were too fresh and painful for him to remain in Niagara Falls, and he packed up his family and moved to what is now Fort Erie. His manor-like home, Bertie Hall, built large to house his 19 children, still stands along Niagara Boulevard. Where did his new fortune come from? Forsyth became a first-rate smuggler (some sources indicate he had been smuggling for his entire adult life), bringing contraband goods across the Niagara River by boat and then selling them to local merchants for a handsome profit. By the time of his death in 1841, he "had established himself as the district's king of smugglers," a notorious criminal who always remained one step ahead of the authorities.

As for the Pavilion, it declined in popularity during the 1830s. Its new owners transformed the grounds into a subdivision of 50-foot lots grandiosely called the City of the Falls. Meanwhile, the Pavilion itself, robbed of its beautiful grounds, tarnished by the acrimonious court cases and run by disinterested owners, lost most of its previous luster. With each passing year, the once-grand hotel faded in importance, as the rich and famous people who formerly found comfort there looked elsewhere for accommodations. By the closing years of the decade, the Pavilion had been superseded by Clifton House, the next generation of luxury hotel and the new place to be seen.

The end for the controversial hotel came on the freezing night of February 19, 1839, when a raging fire, the cause of which was never determined, consumed it in spectacular fashion. Like moths to a flame, dozens of curious onlookers braved the cold to watch in rapt interest as the orange flames devoured the Pavilion.

Samuel DeVeaux was one of those who witnessed the event, and wrote of it later:

> *It continued burning for some time in the evening. The spectacle was grand and solemn. The building was very large and composed entirely of wood. The light reflected upon the rising spray from the Falls, and upon the trees covered with congealed ice. The cloud of mist appeared like another conflagration and to persons at a distance was taken to be such. The ice on the trees reflected back the blazing light, and shone brilliantly in the keen, pure air like*

burning coal. Though thus dazzling, yet it was a sad and painful sight.

It was perhaps fitting that the Pavilion should go out in a blaze of glory. No doubt the founder William Forsyth, ever the showman eager to play to the masses, would have wanted it that way. But the nature of its demise and the shady character of its early owner served to mask the importance of the Pavilion to Niagara Falls' development. It was the first of the luxury hotels, setting the standard of pampering and refinement that continues today in many of the more-expensive hotels. The hotel provided the standard of comfort to which the wealthy were accustomed, and it helped establish Niagara Falls as the premier tourist location in North America.

Not a bad legacy for hotel with such a short and troubled existence.

Maid of the Mist

You feel impossibly small and vulnerable surrounded by waterfalls plummeting from the cliffs towering above you. You can't help but feel awed by the sheer magnificence of the scene, and your camera snaps with a life of its own. The ship inches closer to the cascade, so close that you seem to be almost engulfed in its embrace. A cool mist drenches your poncho and slicks your hair, but you don't mind because directly above you, arched over the deep gorge, is perhaps the most vibrantly colored rainbow you've ever seen. This, you say to yourself, is as close to a heaven-touched experience as you're likely to find on Earth.

The *Maid of the Mist* is, for good reason, Niagara Falls' most famous attraction. Young and old alike love the experience of stepping aboard a boat and sailing to the very base of the falls. It's been a Niagara tradition for more than 160 years.

But the first *Maid of the Mist* boat wasn't built for sightseeing excursions. Instead, it was intended as a hard-working ferry. Until the 1840s, the only way to cross the Niagara was by small rowboats that transported people and goods from one shore to the other. By 1846, however, it became apparent that enough business was to be had that a larger vessel would be profitable, and so a steamboat ferry—christened the *Maid of the Mist*, for a legendary spirit from Native American lore—was launched.

The first steamboat to appear anywhere on the Niagara River, the *Maid* was an inelegant, ungainly barge-like boat, powered by a coal-fired boiler with twin stacks. Few were impressed by her appearance, but this vessel wasn't built for looks; she was built for performance. An entire stagecoach and its team of four horses could be driven right aboard, which meant passengers and cargo could be more efficiently and more safely delivered across the river.

The ferry did well for several years but became obsolete when the Suspension Bridge spanning the river was opened in 1848. To find another source of revenue, the ferry owners began offering sightseeing trips to take tourists upriver to view the falls. The tourist trade flourished, and the vessel did better business in this role than she ever did as a ferry.

George William Curtis, an American writer, felt compelled to commit his memories to paper after an excursion aboard the boat in 1851, which no doubt mirrored the breathless experiences of so many other passengers.

The little steamer leaves the shore by the Suspension Bridge and, gliding with effort into the current of the river, you remember that there is the Cataract on each side. Slowly, slowly tugs the little boat against the stream. Presently comes a puff of cool spray. The fussy little captain exhorts everybody to wrap in a waterproof cloak and cap or else we shall be soaked through and through.

Driving ever closer to the falls, Curtis continued, the *Maid of the Mist* went "straight into the blinding, white, thick, suffocating mist of the Cataract which booms like a steady thunder, cramming the ear with sound...it dances up to the very foot of the Falls. There we tremble in perfect security, mocking with our little *Maid* the might of Niagara." The experience was "a sensation which was equaled nowhere else, the most wonderful water-trip in the world." Indeed, within a matter of years, the *Maid of the Mist* tour had become a world-famous tourist attraction, just as it remains today. The owner recognized, however, that the barge-like boat was not ideally suited to the task. She handled poorly and was slow, didn't provide the level of comfort its wealthy passengers had come to expect and was hardly inspiring to look at. A new *Maid of the Mist*, this one specifically designed for sightseeing excursions, was needed.

In 1854, the second, much larger *Maid of the Mist* was launched. This new vessel was a more luxurious, single-stack paddlewheel steamer, 72 feet long with a draught of eight feet, driven by a powerful 100-horsepower engine. In every way she was superior to her predecessor. And yet, she didn't enjoy the long life of thrilling passengers that was expected.

In 1861, W.O. Buchanon, owner of the *Maid of the Mist*, found himself in dire economic straits and came to the difficult decision of selling the ship at auction. The buyer was a Canadian company that planned to operate her on the St. Lawrence River but with one stipulation to the sale—Buchanon was to be responsible for delivering the ship through the Whirlpool and the Devil's Hole Rapids to Lake Ontario.

It was no easy task. This three-mile stretch of the Niagara River had a dire reputation among mariners, and its white-capped waters are widely considered one of the wildest, most dangerous in the world. Most onlookers considered making the attempt a foolhardy mistake, and even seasoned sailors were certain that the rugged river would swallow the *Maid of the Mist* and anyone aboard.

Buchanon, however, was desperate for the sale to go through, going so far as to offer a princely sum of $500 to the crew that could successfully navigate the ship through the rapids and down to Queenston. No one stepped forward, though, so the task fell to the *Maid of the Mist*'s reluctant skipper, Joel Robinson. The most experienced mariner on the Niagara River, Robinson knew well the dangers of the proposed trip and did not agree to it lightly. But if anyone could succeed, it was he.

Captain Robinson was a legend on the waterway. In 1838, he had taken a small rowboat out into the rapids above the falls to rescue a man marooned on one of the tiny Three Sisters islands. A few years later, he once again ventured into the torrent to save a stranded individual. Witnesses were amazed at Robinson's daring; the islets are just above the falls, a mere stone's throw from the brink, and a single mistake would have sent him plunging over the precipice. And when he became the skipper of the *Maid of the Mist*, he piloted her without incident right up to the edge of the waterfall for more than a decade.

But now Robinson was asked to do the impossible—deliver a fragile paddlewheel steamer through some of the wildest waters imaginable—and he wasn't certain even he was up to the challenge. The money was too good to pass up, however, and he had a reputation for heroics to live up to. In the end, he relented and recruited machinist James McIntyre and engineer James H. Jones to accompany him.

The journey was scheduled for the afternoon of June 15, 1861. Thousands of spectators crowded the shore, well-wishers praying for their safe passage and curious onlookers eager to witness the death-defying spectacle. At 3:00 PM, the *Maid* blew a blast of steam, pulled out into the water and was captured by the powerful current. The little vessel raced down the river and into the rapids, Robinson spinning the wheel desperately to gain some semblance of control over her direction. It was a futile gesture; the crew was at the mercy of the current, reduced to nothing more than bystanders to the unfolding events.

The *Maid of the Mist* was tossed through the rocky waters, waves crashing against her hull and over the deck, causing her to rock dangerously onto her sides. At times, she rolled so much to the side that one of her wheels was completely submerged while the other churned uselessly in the air. Then, suddenly, she dove bow first into a white-capped surge and disappeared from sight. The crowd on shore, hushed, feared she was lost. A moment later, though, the vessel emerged once again, her smoke-stack ripped away but otherwise undamaged.

Now she plunged into the whirlpool. Robinson expertly avoided the vortex at its center and steered the boat from of its swirling grasp. But another, final danger loomed ahead: the Devil's Hole Rapids, "one wild, turbulent rush and whirl of water, without a square foot of smooth surface in the whole distance."

At tremendous speed, the steamer careened through the violent, rock-strewn waters. Waves lashed the hull, the keel ground against the rocks below and the wood seemed to groan under the relentless assault. Robinson was terrified. It sounded as if the ship would be ripped apart at any moment. Incredibly, however, a mere 17 minutes after the perilous journey began, the battered *Maid* and her badly shaken crew anchored at Queenston.

The experience forever changed Robinson. The formerly adventurous and happy-go-lucky man suddenly became cautious and deadly serious. His wife said that he "was twenty years older when he came home that day than when he went out." Though newspapers across the country heralded the trip as the most remarkable ever made by man, Robinson himself saw nothing heroic in it. He vowed never again to venture onto the Niagara River and, what's more, forbade his sons to do so as well. Only two years later, Joel Robinson died.

The *Maid*'s new owners, meanwhile, sailed her across Lake Ontario to the St. Lawrence River and on to Quebec City. There, rechristened the *Maid of Orleans,* she served for many years as a ferry to the Isle of Orleans.

What followed was a long period when visitors to Niagara were deprived of a *Maid of the Mist* experience. In light of the fame and profitability of the early sightseeing boats, it's surprising that, for more than two decades, no one picked up the mantle to built a third *Maid*. It wasn't until 1884 that the service was revived by a pair of enterprising Niagara Falls businessmen, Richard Carter and Frank LeBlond, who together formed the Maid of the Mist Steamboat Company (which still exists and operates the boats today).

The *Maid of the Mist* has been thrilling tourists for more than 160 years. This *Maid*, christened the *Maid of the Mist I* in 1885, is actually the third to bear the world-renowned name.

The third *Maid of the Mist*, a sturdy little boat with none of the elegance and refinement of its predecessor, was launched on June 13, 1884. This boat ventured closer to the Horseshoe Falls than any ever had before, only adding to the novelty and mystique of the experience. Lineups for tickets were so long that it quickly became apparent that a single excursion boat could not possibly cope with the crushing weight of demand. As a result, a sister boat was launched in 1892. In a confusing twist, although they were really the third and fourth vessels to bear the name, the two boats were christened *Maid of the Mist I* and *II.*

Riding aboard the *Maid of the Mist* and viewing the falls from the unique perspective it afforded was as memorable in 1901 as it was half a century earlier, as can clearly be seen in the words of local writer George W. Holley:

> *The admiration which the visitor felt as he passed quietly along near the American Fall was changed into awe when he began to feel the mighty pulse of the great deep just below the tower, then swung round into the white foam directly in front of the Horseshoe, and saw the sky of waters falling toward him. And he seemed to be lifted on wings as he sailed swiftly down the rushing stream through a baptism of spray.*

These twin boats served for more than six decades and likely would have continued had fate not intervened. On April 22, 1955, as the *Maids* were undergoing routine maintenance in preparation for the coming season, a spark from a welder's torch set both ablaze. Desperate attempts to save the vessels were in vain, so that when the flames eventually died, the boats were left as burned-out hulks. Attempts to preserve the fire-ravaged boats similarly failed; they were too far gone and had to be wrecked.

But this time, Niagara Falls did not have to wait 20 years without a *Maid of the Mist*. A 40-foot yacht called *The Little Maid* was hastily built in the spring of 1955 to save the operating season, but a new *Maid of the Mist* was launched later that summer and a second the following June. Two more have followed since.

Today, the *Maid of the Mist* continues to thrill visitors as one of North America's oldest tourist attractions. For more than 150 years, some of them marked by unforgettable moments, the various boats that have taken the famous name have sailed awe-struck passengers through the swirling waters and into the magical mists. It's almost impossible now to imagine Niagara Falls without a *Maid of the Mist* with which to explore the roaring cascade.

Whirlpool Aero Car

After the falls themselves, the most frequently visited and awe-inspiring spot on the Niagara River is almost certainly the Whirlpool, a unique geological formation of primal fury. The racing waters form a swirling, white-capped vortex that's both frightening to behold and yet oddly alluring. Though spectacular even from a safe distance along the river banks, the best way to appreciate this natural wonder is from the confines of the Aero Car that crosses the 1800-foot-wide gorge, offering a bird's eye view from some 250 feet above the tempestuous waters.

Although to modern eyes the Aero Car looks quaint, perhaps even dangerously outdated, at the time of its construction, it was a marvel of engineering and incorporated the latest in scientific thought. It was the brain-child of brilliant Spanish engineer Leonardo Torres-Quevado, a man who for all his scientific genius is little known today. Born in 1852, he began his career by overseeing the construction of railway lines in southern Spain, later devoting his energy to more cutting-edge technology. For example, he pioneered work in calculators and computers and designed an improved dirigible system that was an important step forward for blimps. But for all his vast body of work, the Aero Car at Niagara was the one with the greatest legacy. It was, quite simply, his crowning glory.

In 1913, Torres-Quevado and a group of wealthy investors formed the Spanish Aero Car Company with the expressed purpose of building a cable car across Niagara's Whirlpool Gorge. It was a daunting task—many thought it impossible—but Torres-Quevado was confident he had the solution and,

together with other partners, he approached the
Niagara Parks Commission for permission to proceed. After a careful study of the plans, permission
was granted, and in 1914 work began on what soon
became one of the region's signature attractions.

The Whirlpool Aero Car has been a Niagara attraction
since 1916. Passengers get a bird's-eye view of a Niagara
attraction of even older vintage, the Whirlpool, the bar
against which 19th-century daredevils measured their
bravery, and supposedly the home of a legendary monster.

By the summer of 1916, just in time to take advantage of the tourist season, the Aero Car was complete. It was the first of its kind anywhere in the world, the safest cable car in existence. The car rides on six lock coil track cables, the tensions of which are independent of the weight of the car, due to counterweights at the end of each cable. As a result, if one cable breaks, there is absolutely no danger to the car or its passengers, because the other cables do not have an increase in load. The price tag for this marvel was $120,000, a vast sum of money in those days.

The official ribbon-cutting ceremony took place on August 8, 1916. Several hundred enthusiastic guests were on hand for the event, each one excited and perhaps a bit nervous at the prospect of being among the first to ride in the new contraption. The proud inventor, Leonardo Torres-Quevado, was present at the ceremony and clearly was delighted by the reaction to his cable car (it was to be the only time he saw it in action; he did not return to Niagara before his 1936 death).

Shortly after three o'clock, Mrs. J. Enoch Thompson, the wife of the Spanish Consul in Toronto, broke a bottle of champagne over the car's gate. As the glass shattered, an enthusiastic cheer erupted from the crowd. And then, needing little coaxing, six people stepped forward for the honor of being the first to ride over the Whirlpool.

At that time, and for many years after, passengers could get on or off the Aero Car at either side. Eventually, it was decided that there should only be one point of entrance and exit. The reason? To foil scam artists preying on gullible passengers. The con men, no doubt struggling to suppress smiles, told people that they could get them illegally into the United States by way of the Aero Car, for a fee, of course. They were breaking the law, after all, and had to be compensated for the risk. The victims were then ushered aboard the car and told that, as soon as it reached the other side, they were in America and should jump off and run. This they did, not realizing, of course, that they were actually still in Canada.

The Aero Car has delighted visitors to Niagara for almost a century, and though it has been operated over the years by various private interests, the Niagara Parks Commission has owned and controlled it since 1969. It has a perfect safety record, but sadly, that's not to say the cable car has not seen tragedy.

On the morning of Sunday, August 12, 1934, Ruth Hyde of Bradford, Pennsylvania, visited the Whirlpool. She didn't come to marvel at the natural spectacle, as countless others do, but rather came troubled and with a determination to end her misery.

Ruth was a sad and lonely woman. She had wealth beyond her wildest dreams; her husband, oil tycoon William P. Hyde, saw to that. But she wasn't happy. Her husband, at 87, was more than 50 years older than her—so no children were in Ruth's future. William was also old-fashioned, conservative and, because of his advanced age, largely confined to home. Ruth felt trapped, imprisoned in a cycle of boredom and drudgery. Suddenly, her life had become an inescapable nightmare. In her mind, she had only one option.

On Saturday, August 11, Ruth announced to her husband that she was going to visit friends in Brookville, Pennsylvania, where she had lived prior to her marriage two years earlier. She said she would return the next day.

Instead of going to Brookville, Ruth drove toward Niagara Falls, New York. The next morning, Sunday, she hired taxi driver William Groom to take her on a sightseeing tour. At the end of the drive, Ruth thanked the driver and said, cryptically, that "the river has an awful fascination for me." It seems she had in mind an escape from her tortured prison.

Around 3:30 that afternoon, Ruth hired another cab to take her to the Aero Car. Upon arriving, she paid the driver, gave him a sweet smile and instructed him not to wait for her. She then bought a ticket for the Aero Car. As she was boarding, she gave her purse to the operator, Harold Brooker, to hold onto until the ride was over. She was concerned about dropping it, she said.

Ruth took her seat among the other passengers. Arthur McKinley, accompanying his six-year-old daughter, Catherine, took note of the attractive woman seated directly across from him. He later recalled that she was "a pretty woman with bright red hair and light complexion. She wore a reddish plaid dress." Nothing in the woman's appearance or actions gave McKinley any hint as to what was about to take place.

The ride began. Nothing untoward happened until the car was directly over the roiling center of the Whirlpool. McKinley noticed that the woman across from him suddenly became nervous, almost agitated. Her hands shook visibly, her face was ashen, and she had a tearful look in her eyes. She lit a cigarette to calm her nerves. McKinley assumed, and later regretted it, that the woman was simply afraid of heights and was having trouble coping with the dizzying vertigo. He had no idea how wrong he was.

Ruth was indeed scared. Shudders of fear rippled through her; taking your own life is difficult to do, even when misery clouds your mind. But Ruth knew she could not go back to her existence. Every day spent living that joyless life seemed to drive her deeper into a blinding depression. She had no recourse, her mind was made up. She suddenly stood, threw away her cigarette and, before the startled passengers even knew what was happening, climbed onto her seat and leaped over the safety gate. It all happened so fast that no one had a chance to react. When the passengers leaned over the sides of the car and searched the swirling waters, they saw no sign of Ruth. She likely died on impact, her body then sucked into the vortex and from view.

Four days later, the U.S. Coastguard off Youngstown, New York, recovered Ruth's body, with most of her clothing ripped away by the current. Police, meanwhile, had already conducted their investigation. When Ruth's purse was opened, they discovered her identity and a letter addressed to her husband outlining her intention to end her life. When contacted, William Hyde was stunned and could offer no reason why his wife would commit suicide. With no evidence of wrongdoing, the case was closed and Ruth Hyde forgotten, just another one of the hundreds of tragic figures who have taken their own lives at Niagara.

Although the Aero Car was used to take a life in that instance, it also once saved one during a dramatic rescue. In 1949, Major Lloyd Hill, the son of Niagara river man and daredevil William "Red" Hill Sr., decided he wanted to write himself into the history books. His father had made a 1930 trip through the Whirlpool in a barrel emblazoned with the letters, "William Red Hill, Master Hero of Niagara." In 1942, his brother, 19-year-old Red Jr., had also taken the thrilling journey and repeated it six years later. Major was not about to be the only

Hill who had not braved the mighty Niagara. It was a matter of pride.

Major designed a steel barrel equipped with fins worked by levers that were intended, so he said, to allow himself to steer through the Whirlpool. Most onlookers scoffed at the notion, but he was confident his contraption would give him a degree of control enjoyed by no previous daredevil who had ridden a barrel through the Whirlpool. He would be proven wrong.

The barrel entered the Whirlpool and, despite the addition of the fins, quickly became trapped in the circling maelstrom. For two hours, the raging current battered and bruised Major, who was sometimes thrown as high as 40 feet in the air by the pounding waves. No one knew how long he could endure the beating. Major was finally rescued in a spectacular fashion by being hauled up with ropes dangling from the Aero Car above. Not to be dissuaded, however, Major subsequently made three successful rides through the rapids, in 1950, 1954 and 1956.

Thankfully, most of the millions of people who have ridden the Aero Car have had a more pleasurable experience than did either Ruth Hyde or Major Lloyd Hill. Visitors thrill at the adventure of gliding across the gorge suspended by only six cables that seem impossibly thin for the load borne, and they marvel at the wild waters seething with pent-up fury below. Cameras snap, people point excitedly and smiles spread across faces.

One can almost imagine the spirit of Leonardo Torres-Quevado looking on with pride, thrilled that his invention has become one of the most beloved attractions at Niagara Falls, as popular today as it was when he was on hand for its unveiling almost 100 years ago in 1916.

CHAPTER SEVEN

Villains and Scoundrels

NIAGARA FALLS BILLS ITSELF as the "Honeymoon Capital of the World." The inference is obvious: it's a place of romance, of beauty, a magical place infused with excitement and warmth. The rare kind of locale where dreams really do become reality.

For most of the thousands who bask in the glow of newlywed bliss, with the falls roaring in the background, and indeed for the millions who visit every year during family vacations, Niagara Falls lives up to its reputation. But there's a darker side to the place, a history suppressed lest it ruin the atmosphere. For, over the years, Niagara Falls has been home to more than its share of unredeemable villains: murderers, traitors, terrorists, con men and rogues.

Some villains emerged during the turmoil and chaos of war. John Willcocks was a well-known traitor who literally set the Niagara region alight during the War of 1812. Even worse was Benjamin Lett, a fiery-tempered and utterly ruthless Irishman who sided with the revolutionaries during the ill-fated Rebellion of 1837. His list of atrocities was long and diverse, and for years the mere mention of his name caused fear among area residents.

Greed motivated other villains. During the 1800s, many sought to profit in an underhanded way from the tourists who flocked to the falls. Swindlers were aplenty, and by mid-century, Niagara was quickly falling into disrepute. Among the thriving criminal element, none was worse than Saul Davis, whose Table Rock Hotel was known as the "Cave of Forty Thieves," for the way its proprietor and his thuggish sons extorted money from visitors.

Things got so bad that, in 1873, a Royal Commission was established to clean up Niagara Falls, and gradually the worst elements were weeded out. But, still, disreputable characters surfaced every now and then. There was Arthur Hoyt Day, for example, who threw his wife into the gorge because he could no longer afford two wives and decided one had to be eliminated. He was hanged for his crime. So too was Lenny Jackson, a Niagara-born gangster who ran with the notorious Boyd Gang in the 1940s and '50s during their remarkable string of bank robberies.

And surely there were many others, individuals whose crimes have long since been forgotten or erased from public consciousness by a community eager to put their misdeeds out of sight and out of mind.

This rogue's gallery of unsavory individuals is an embarrassment to Niagara Falls. They represent the worst of humanity: self-indulgence in the extreme, ruthless violence, the seeking of gain with a complete disregard for the rights and well-being of others. Niagara's villains represent dark stain in the area's history, but no one can deny they make for gripping storytelling.

An Unsavory Spectacle: The *Michigan*

During much of the 19th century, a dark stain spread on Niagara Falls in an infamous area of disrepute known as the Front. This notorious quarter-mile strip ran from Table Rock to Clifton House and was a haven for every conceivable manner of vice and villainy. Gamblers, pickpockets, con men and swindlers, "soiled doves," thugs and, the biggest scoundrels of them all, the proprietors of the half-dozen hotels, competed tooth and nail for patrons.

The early hotelkeepers were an unsavory, opportunistic lot who used every means possible, legal and illegal, even immoral, to make a profit. But in the fall of 1827, three hoteliers sunk to new lows when they organized what was the earliest and the cruelest publicity stunt in Niagara Falls' history. Sending a derelict ship, the *Michigan*, full of helpless, caged animals over the falls demonstrated the depths to which these individuals, driven by greed and unhindered by morality, would go in the never-ending quest to make money.

At any one time, between four and six hotels were in the Front, all operated in much the same fashion. They overcharged for rooms, demanded payment for services that were advertised as free and watered down the alcohol. But it was an unwise guest who complained or refused to pay up; hotelkeepers kept foul and surly thugs on hand to deal rather violently with troublemakers. One visitor who protested at the unspecified charges added to his bill was thrown through a glass door, then grabbed by the throat and hurled to the ground, where his pockets were rifled for the money owed. It was best just to pay up and be done with it.

Complicit in the scamming were hack drivers (as carriage drivers were then known), who hustled unwary tourists to whatever hotel paid their commission, regardless of the wishes of the passengers. Once at the destination, passengers were forced out and their luggage dropped, then the hack was quickly wheeled away. The passengers had little option but to accept the accommodations before them.

Proprietors knew who to target. Americans were the victim of choice; they lived hundreds of miles away and could neither afford the time nor the money to launch a civil suit against them. And even if the victim was inclined to seek justice, it probably wouldn't have changed the shady character of the Front. After all, you couldn't point fingers at just one hotelkeeper; they were all just as bad.

Perhaps that's not true. Some were probably worse than others. John Brown, proprietor of the Ontario House, was among the most opportunistic of the lot, but he got away with it because he had impeccable political connections. William Forsyth, a bitter rival, operated the elegant Pavilion Hotel that catered to upper-class clientele. (For more information on William Forsyth and the Pavilion, see Chapter Six: Tourism Comes to Niagara.) But don't let the refinement of his establishment fool you; if anything, Forsyth was even more opportunistic than Brown, and that was saying something. These competitors, who held a deep-seated disdain for one another, pushed aside their mutual animosity to plan a publicity stunt designed to lure visitors to Niagara Falls in unprecedented numbers. Joining them was a third hotelkeeper, General Parkhurst Whitney, who operated the Eagle Tavern on the American side.

Together, in 1827, the threesome dreamed up a stunt that was spectacular and tasteless. They purchased a rotting and condemned 16-foot schooner, the *Michigan,* and planned to outfit it as a pirate vessel, complete with effigies of buccaneers serving as her crew of cutthroats. The vessel would also be filled with a cargo of "wild and ferocious animals" and then sent hurdling over Horseshoe Falls.

Posters advertising the event made it sound like good fun:

The greatest exertions are making [sic] to procure Animals of the ferocious kind, such as panthers, wild cats, bears, and wolves; but in lieu of some of these, which it may be impossible to obtain, a few

vicious or worthless dogs, such as may possess con-
siderable strength and activity, and perhaps a few of
the toughest of the lesser animals, will be added to,
and compose, the cargo....

To make the event more appealing to women and children, the poster went on to say, "should the animals be young and hardy, and possessed of great muscular powers, and joining their fate with that of the vessel, remain on board till she reaches the waters below, there is great possibility that many of them, will have performed the terrible jaunt, unhurt." Of course, the promoters knew full well that the animals would perish, but it made them seem less bloodthirsty if people were made to believe the animals had a chance at survival.

The promoters went further by even suggesting that the *Michigan*, if she steered through the deepest water of the river, had a good chance of surviving the drop down the falls intact. It was all part of building up expectations and adding a sense of drama. Some people even naively believed the claims.

Though it was full of hyperbole, the advertising certainly worked. On September 8, the biggest crowd yet seen in Niagara converged on the falls; estimates range from 10,000 to 30,000 people were on hand to witness what was billed as a "remarkable spectacle unequalled in the annals of infernal navigation."

It was a rogue's dream. With so many people to prey upon, thieves and scoundrels of every type were promised an easy fortune. Gamblers brought their wheels of fortune; buskers and peddlers hounded visitors; cutpurses and pickpockets slunk through the crowd eager to relieve targets of the burden of their coin; and disreputable women called out to gentlemen passersby.

At three o'clock in the afternoon, the show everyone had been eagerly anticipating finally began. The *Michigan* was towed from Black Rock to Navy Island and then to a point just above the rapids, where she was cut loose. A cheer erupted from the crowds pressed up against the river shore. Some people, wanting to get a better view, even climbed trees or sat on rooftops. The mood was electric.

Aboard the boat, however, the atmosphere was decidedly different. As the *Michigan* picked up speed and raced through the rapids, bobbing crazily as it pounded against wave and rock, the animals began to panic. Some people ashore even claimed to hear their cries above the roar of the water. The imprisoned animals were a pathetic bunch, hardly living up to the billing: two sad-looking bears, an almost infirm buffalo, two foxes, a raccoon, an eagle, a dog and 15 geese. They were hardly the ferocious beasts that had been promised.

It wasn't long before the *Michigan*'s mast was lost, torn away like a twig. Shortly after, and before the ship had even reached the crest of the falls, her hull began to break apart. The bears and buffalo managed to break free and jump overboard, swimming desperately for shore. Incredibly, one bear made it, crawling on shaky legs to reach Goat Island, where it was later caught and put on display. Meanwhile, the decrepit schooner broke in half moments before she was to tumble over the precipice. Only splinters of wood survived the fall. A lone goose that took flight as the ship plummeted to her doom was the sole survivor among the remaining animals.

The results exceeded the promoters' wildest expectations. Hotel rooms were booked full to overflowing, and so much alcohol was consumed that their entire stock was depleted, and still many people went thirsty. The promoters raked in the money hand over fist.

But most spectators were left sadly disappointed by the pitiful entertainment. Expecting to see a menagerie of savage, exotic beasts, they instead got a motley crew of animals, some of which were more at home in a barnyard than in the wilderness. The crowd had wanted to see a fearsome pirate vessel and ideally to watch it emerge from the mists below the falls in one piece. Instead, the promoters provided a rotting ship that bore no resemblance to a terror of the high seas and certainly had no chance of surviving a plunge over the falls. And the spectators had hoped to cheer as animals swam ashore unharmed at the end of the show, having completed the "terrible jaunt." As a result, most left disillusioned and feeling as though they'd been swindled.

Although Niagara's hotel proprietors never again staged another show this ambitious, they continued to hustle their guests and add new scams to their bag of tricks. For example, hotels sold sulfur water from the totally fictitious Burning Springs, said to be located a short distance up river. The water was actually taken from the river and was completely normal, but gullible guests purchased it in the belief that it had healing properties. Also available for sale were bottles containing, if you can believe it, "congealed spray" from the cataract!

It was another half-century before Niagara's hotelkeepers and other criminal elements were forced to clean up their act—but only after the unsavory reputation of the Front had stained Niagara Falls as a whole and made tourism suffer. Hoteliers had no choice but to become reputable or be driven from town. Their days of ruthlessly exploiting tourists were at an end.

Benjamin Lett

BENJAMIN LETT WAS A brutal, quick-tempered outlaw who terrorized the Niagara region for more than a decade in the mid-1800s and never hesitated to spill blood. People were afraid to even speak against him, lest he arrive at their door one night with a pistol in one hand, knife in the other and murder in his eyes. The British government was desperate to bring his reign of fear to an end, one way or the other. And even though most Ontario newspapers condemned his criminal activity, they nonetheless delighted in running stories about him, because violence and scandal, then as now, sold copies.

Lett was public enemy number one in Canada, with a string of assassinations, bombings and acts of sabotage to his name. He spread panic and anarchy across Niagara, determined to strike a mortal blow against the British colonial government. Today, he would rightly be branded a terrorist.

No one knows for certain where Lett's burning hatred of the British originated. He was born in Ireland in 1814, and some accounts suggest English soldiers had raped his mother during the endless cycle of violence that wracked the island. We do know that this violence cost Lett his uncle, his mother's brother, who was viciously murdered in 1798. The family moved to Canada in 1819 and settled on a farmstead just east of Toronto, where, just a few short years later, Lett's father died in a tragic accident. Misfortune, which had plagued the family for so long, suddenly turned its attention elsewhere, and for the next two decades the family lived a quiet and by all accounts contented life.

Nevertheless, something unsettling simmered in Benjamin beneath the surface, building to a boil. He had a quick temper, was unpredictable—one minute bright and cheerful, the next moody and dark—and some neighbors described him as being "a dangerous, queer man to have a difference with." Most observers doubtlessly would have agreed that Benjamin was eventually bound to erupt. It was not a question of if, but when, and under what circumstances.

The simmer came to a boil in 1837, a year of rebellion and political crisis in Upper Canada (Ontario), during which Lett was driven onto a path of murder and mayhem.

For years, William Lyon Mackenzie had led a campaign in the Legislature and within the columns of his own newspaper, the *Colonial Advocate,* agitating for political reform. By early 1837, he began to despair of the Reformer movement making any headway against the corrupt colonial government at York. He and his followers—and there were many—started to prepare for the time when force might be required to make their point heard.

Into this delicate situation came Sir Francis Bond Head, the new lieutenant-governor of Upper Canada and a vainglorious man devoid of either common sense or political subtlety. By year's end he managed to infuriate the Reformers, polarize the province into two opposing camps and add tinder to an already incendiary situation. Rebellion, threatened in hushed tones for years, was now inevitable. The pent-up fury finally erupted into rebellion in early December as a rag-tag army of insurgents marched toward Toronto and the seat of Upper Canada's government there.

Benjamin Lett was soon swept up by the currents of revolution. Soon after Mackenzie's army was dispersed at the Battle of Montgomery's Tavern, a loyalist posse rode into the Lett farm and demanded that Benjamin join them in hunting down suspected rebels. The Irishman refused; although he took no part in the rebellion, he sympathized with their cause and certainly felt no loyalty to King and Country. Lett's refusal cast suspicion upon him, and the posse arrested him. But while being transported to prison in Kingston, he managed to escape from his three guards, "overpowering them by sheer strength and cunning...." Lett fled into the woods with musket balls shredding bark all around him.

Now being hunted, Lett headed to New York State and joined the exiled rebels hiding there. He joined a band of militant and radical revolutionaries called the Patriot Hunters, or simply Patriots, and began a career of terror that included bombings, intimidation and assassination. The rebels crossed the Niagara River for a single night's ill-deeds, their attacks calculated to arouse fear, disrupt commerce and incite a war between the United States and Britain that they hoped would end with American victory and the independence of Canada.

The vast majority of their misdeeds were relatively minor, involving threatening letters, robberies, beatings, barn burnings and murdering of cattle. Some, however, were far more heinous, and invariably these carried the dark signature of Benjamin Lett. The crime that solidified Lett's reputation for extremism and brutality occurred during darkness on November 16, 1838.

The moon was partially hidden behind rows of low-lying clouds, peeking out every now and then to illuminate the landscape for a few moments in dim silvery light. A gentle breeze passed through the fields, the rustle of the cool winds helping to muffle Lett's footfalls as he glided silently toward the Chippawa home of Captain Edgeworth Ussher, a noted British loyalist. Lett had not picked his target at random; years earlier, Captain Ussher had commanded a small party of men who crossed the Niagara River to board and burn the rebel schooner, *Caroline*. Selecting this respected military man as a target for assassination, an individual hailed locally as a hero, would be an act of retribution and would surely send a powerful message.

Lett may have been musing on this when a dog suddenly barked in the distance, shattering the night's stillness. Lett lowered himself to the ground and pressed his body flat, waiting motionless for long moments until the barking stopped. He only resumed his advance once he saw no signs of activity in Ussher's home.

Lett left the field and approached the home, walking with silent steps over a carpet of decaying leaves. With a pair of pistols in his hands, he climbed onto the porch and disrupted the silence by rapping loudly on the door. The knocks echoed through the night, causing the dog in the distance to resume his howling.

Captain Ussher awoke at the sound. His wife, Sally, stirred beside him. Ussher lit a candle, slipped from his bed and pulled on a robe. His wife, now alert as well, begged him not to answer the door. The string of nighttime assaults on people and property at the hands of the Patriot Hunters had her on edge, and she knew her husband's pro-British sentiments made him a target of retribution. But Ussher would not be cowed; he went to answer the door to prove he couldn't be intimidated.

The rapping at the door was more urgent now, as Ussher peeked in on his four children, lying fearful in their beds, blankets pulled tight to their chins. Ussher urged them back to sleep then descended the stairs and made his way across the hall. The door opened, and two shots rang out in the blackness. Ussher caught the bullets full in his chest, the balls of lead shattering his ribcage and organs. He fell to the ground as his shadowy assailant disappeared into the gloom. When Sally arrived at her husband's side moments later, his eyes were glassy and his fingers twitched uncontrollably, the flame of life all but extinguished. The soon-to-be widow cried and screamed, and somewhere in the darkness of the night Benjamin Lett smiled.

In the days after the brutal murder, the Canadian government offered a substantial reward for Lett's capture. The *St. Catharines Journal* believed that by this "most deliberate, unprovoked and cold-blooded assassination...no man is safe! Every responsible inhabitant...must rise up as one man to put down the atrocity of such lawless fiends in the form of men." The *Niagara Courier* stated that Captain Ussher's murder was "but the introductory act of a reign of terror" perpetrated by "a mystick [sic] brotherhood of ruffians who have bound themselves in a secret oath for purposes of plunder and revenge in Canada." Terror gripped Niagara, and people began to wonder who would be targeted next.

Lett and his followers reveled in the perceived victory. A poem boasting of the murder, entitled "On the Execution of Captain Ussher," and proba-bly written by the terrorist's own hand, appeared in the Lockport, New York, *Freeman's Advocate*. Here was a man who didn't just kill out of some twisted sense of duty but, more importantly, because he enjoyed the notoriety and attention his thuggish exploits generated. Ussher's assassination was not the only crime in which Lett became implicated. In January 1839, he made an unsuccessful attempt to burn a British ship at Kingston. Six months later, he was implicated in a failed raid on the town of Cobourg. Lett's lack of success left him frustrated and full of self-doubt by the year's end. He needed to make a spectacular statement in 1840, some-thing that would shake the enemy and bolster the faltering spirits of the Patriots. To achieve that, Lett elected to strike at what was then one of Canada's most recognizable symbols, the monument to War of 1812 hero General Isaac Brock.

Brock was a martyr, having sacrificed his life to secure victory at the Battle of Queenston Heights and, more importantly in the eyes of most Canadians, to save the nation from American occupation. He was Canada's first hero, an instant legend, and his remains were buried beneath a 135-foot-tall monument built atop the very bluff where he fell mortally wounded on October 12, 1812. Lett struck against this revered edifice on Good Friday, April 17, 1840. The peace and tranquility of that sacred day were shattered by rumbling echoes rolling down from atop Queenston Heights, and when people went to investigate, they found the Brock Monument defiled. A powerful bomb had exploded inside the base of the memorial, shattering the staircase, blowing off part of the peak and cracking the column. Canadians were outraged; Lett and his followers rejoiced.

Perhaps overconfident in the wake of this resounding success, Lett made a clumsy and ill-planned attempt in June 1840 to burn a steamship at Oswego, New York. Caught in the act, he was arrested, promptly convicted of arson and sentenced to seven years of hard labor at the Auburn, New York, prison. Lett had no intention of languishing behind bars, however. En route to prison, he managed to break free from his guards, jump down a 20-foot embankment and escape into the woods.

The embarrassed and enraged governor of New York offered a huge reward for Lett's capture. Those attempting to apprehend him were urged to proceed with caution; Lett was considered armed (he carried four loaded pistols and two large knives with him at all times) and, as a result of his devil-may-care attitude, extremely dangerous.

Lett was now wanted on both sides of the border and had no safe haven. Yet, he remained at large for more than a year, thanks in large part to the shelter and support provided by his rebel compatriots, but he was finally recaptured in Buffalo in September 1841. Escorted to prison by a large party of heavily armed police, he was thrown into solitary confinement where, in the darkness and solitude, he had years on end to reflect on his violent, murderous ways. According to his brother Thomas, Lett was regularly beaten by the guards, crippling his body and spirit.

During Lett's incarceration, the tenor of the times had changed. The British government had offered amnesty to most rebels, including leaders such as William Lyon Mackenzie, and had taken steps to address most of their complaints by making extensive reforms in the political and economic realms. As a result, there was no longer any appetite for revolution, and Lett's former allies distanced themselves from him and other radicals like him.

After four years behind bars, his health shattered by poor conditions and abuse, Lett was pardoned by New York Governor Silas Wright. The years in prison had dampened his appetite for revolution, and instead of continuing his personal crusade against the British, he went to live with his siblings on a farm near Northville, Illinois. There he lived in obscurity; he didn't talk much about his past, and his acquaintances didn't ask a lot of questions. It was a quiet life, but it apparently suited him.

But his violent past eventually caught up with him. In December 1858, while involved in a trading expedition on Lake Michigan, Lett suddenly became violently ill. He was raced by steamship to Milwaukee but faded quickly and, despite the doctor's best efforts, died nine days later. An autopsy indicated death by strychnine poisoning. Thomas Lett and many other observers were certain British agents were responsible for what was clearly murder.

But few mourned his passing. Benjamin Lett was one of the most feared individuals in Canada, a dangerous radical, a wildcat willing to murder anyone who stood in his path, a man who reveled in sowing the seeds of chaos. To most Canadians, and especially those in Niagara, he was a despicable villain who deserved to die. Although they might have preferred that he die at the end of a rope after a trial, death by poison was preferable to allowing the terrorist to go free.

In the end, Benjamin Lett died just as he had lived: violently. And with news of his passing, Niagara breathed a sigh of relief.

Arthur Hoyt Day

A howling wind cut easily through the young man's jacket, tussling his perfectly combed hair and pulling free the flower jauntily tucked into his lapel. He reflexively reached to brush his hair back into place, but the chains binding his wrists pulled him up short. His eyes scanned the crowd pressing in on him, noting the almost eager looks etched on their faces and the easy manner in which they spoke to one another. Arthur Hoyt Day didn't share their light mood. How could he, with the ominous shape of the gallows looming before him?

The condemned man solemnly climbed the stairs, silently praying that God would have enough mercy on him—despite the heinous nature of his crime—to grant him a quick and painless death. And in that moment, perhaps he wondered for the first time whether his murdered wife had suffered in her dying moments.

You would have liked Arthur Hoyt Day. Everybody did. Tall, charming and handsome, he was the kind of guy other men were happy to share a few beers with, and he was a favorite with the ladies. About the only people who weren't taken with him were the police, who knew Day as a troublemaker and rogue.

Born in Rochester, New York, in 1864, Arthur Hoyt Day was raised in a family who collectively had little respect for the law. His sister, Mary, for a time ran a brothel in Lockport, New York, and had been arrested several times for minor felonies. Three of his brothers spent considerable time behind bars in federal penitentiaries for far worse. By 1890, Arthur himself had caught the attention of the police several times, and, though he was gainfully employed as a hotel clerk, few had any illusions that he had suddenly reformed his ways.

In 1884, 20-year-old Arthur Hoyt Day wed Desiree Chatterton. She was a domestic servant several years his senior and was a plain woman, but she had her uses: she kept his house and made his meals. The marriage was more of an arrangement than a union of love, and pretty soon it got ugly. It wasn't long before rumors emerged that Arthur abused his wife.

The trouble with Desiree, as far as Arthur was concerned, was that she was dull. She wasn't anything to look at, she was hard-working but hardly exciting, and she was simple in her ways. Clearly unsatisfied with Desiree, he began to cast about for more thrilling female companionship, moonlighting as Arthur Hoyt. Always well-dressed despite his modest occupation, he presented himself as a gentleman and never had trouble finding women to share his nights. We'll never know if Desiree suspected his infidelity, but his job as a porter, with its unpredictable hours and numerous nighttime shifts, was the perfect cover.

In 1890, Arthur met a beautiful woman named Mary Breen. The two began a passionate affair, though in her defense, Mary had no idea her lover was married. Arthur was smitten. This was the woman, he told himself, that he should be with. She looked great on his arm, was full of life and there was something exciting about her. Eventually he asked himself why he couldn't be with Mary. The fact that he was already married didn't seem reason enough, so Arthur proposed to Mary and she gleefully accepted. On July 12, they were wed in Canandaigua.

Somehow, Arthur juggled two wives for a few weeks without either one of them growing suspicious, but the strain was wearing on him. Racing between two households, keeping lies straight, supporting two wives...it was harder than he had imagined it would be. Arthur knew he couldn't keep the charade up for long, so he came to the conclusion that one of his women would have to go. Plain Desiree was the obvious choice.

On Sunday, July 27, 1890, Arthur took Desiree and his sister, Mary Quigley, to Niagara Falls for what was to be, he told them, several days of cheerful sightseeing. The two women were excited to see the attractions, and Arthur was excited too, because he knew when he returned there would be only one Mrs. Arthur Hoyt Day. It was all part of his sinister plan.

It was mid-afternoon when the three of them began walking along the river toward the Whirlpool. Growing tired, Mary decided to sit down on a rock to rest while her brother and his wife carried on. They eventually came to a stop several hundred feet away and at the very edge of the gorge. The couple stood there for a while, soaking in the breathtaking view. Mary's attention was drawn away for a moment, and when she looked back, Arthur was alone.

Mary bolted to her feet and raced to her brother's side.

"Where's Desiree?" she asked, instinctively knowing the truth.

"I pushed her off the cliff," Arthur said calmly. "I wanted to get rid of her."

Arthur then ordered his badly shaken sister not to go to the police, handed her a train ticket to return home and then walked away. It wasn't until three days later that Arthur reappeared in Rochester and got in touch with Mary. It was only then that Arthur revealed to his sister that he had secretly married another woman several weeks earlier and told her he felt only slight regret for killing poor Desiree. He then reminded his sister of her promise not to go to the police.

Mary was true to her word, but Arthur had graver concerns. His new wife, Mary Breen, started to have some concerns about the man she had married. For one thing, he kept talking in his sleep, saying such things as, "There she goes, over." Sometimes he would bolt upright in his sleep, point at an imaginary object, and cry out, "See, there she is now!" The outbursts could be excused as nothing more than nightmares, but they a suggested a troubled mind and made her suspicious.

Worse, Mary Breen heard rumors that Arthur was already married, and she noticed laundry tags on some of his clothes that bore the name Arthur Day. No longer having any doubt in her mind that she shared her husband with another woman, she went to the police and had Arthur arrested for bigamy.

But now a problem arose. No one could locate the first wife. Detectives Kavanagh and Furtherer searched all of Rochester and many neighboring communities for Desiree but came up empty. A pattern of suspicion was forming, and the detectives were convinced that foul play was involved. They decided to dig deeper and brought Mary Quigley in for questioning. She had no intention of sharing in Arthur's guilt, so it took little to convince her to break her vow of silence and relate the events of July 27 in all of its grim entirety.

Mary even volunteered to return to Niagara Falls with detectives and lead them to the exact spot where Desiree had been pushed off the cliff into the gorge below. It had been almost two weeks since the murder was committed, so when the corpse was located on the rocks, it was already badly decomposed and partially eaten by scavengers. But with a corpse in evidence, and Mary Quigley willing to testify, officers could now charge Arthur with murder.

When Arthur Hoyt Day was arrested, he was overcome with grief, but few were convinced by the act. Matters proceeded rapidly from that point. Though both the accused and the victim were American citizens, the crime had occurred on Canadian soil and therefore the trial was to take place in Canada. Arthur was duly extradited and taken to a jail in Welland. He was surprisingly calm even behind bars. The Watertown, New York, *Daily News* for October 7 noted that, "since his imprisonment, Day has taken his arrest and the awful charges against him very lightly." He was clearly confident of an acquittal.

Large crowds converged on the town of Welland for the trial, and when the proceedings finally began, the courtroom was jammed with spectators. Hundreds of others who had hoped to watch the proceedings had to be turned away. When Arthur appeared, he was impeccably dressed, including a red flower in his coat lapel. "He is good looking and dresses stylishly," noted the *Watertown Daily News*. Although most in the crowd hissed, some women were impressed with his youthful good looks and seemed to forget the heinous nature of the crime.

As expected, Arthur pleaded not guilty to the charges. His initial testimony was that he had no idea what had happened to Desiree. They had argued, he said, and he left his angered wife alongside the river. Arthur claimed not to know how his wife had ended up at the bottom of a rocky gorge, though he suggested perhaps she had slipped while picking berries.

Mary Quigley was an early sensation in the witness box as she testified against her brother. The Crown's case depended heavily on her statement, and the defense tried to discredit her because of her past. Arthur's attorneys called into question her character by noting she had been married four times and had been arrested on numerous occasions. They also honed in on her time as a brothel madam. Indeed, Arthur went so far as to point a finger at his sister, blaming her for Desiree's death. He claimed Mary had heavily drugged his wife with alcohol and perhaps even arsenic that day, and that it was she who had pushed Desiree over the edge.

Arthur's impassioned but implausible testimony aside, the trial's outcome was never really in doubt. No one was surprised when the jury came back with a guilty verdict. No one but Arthur, that is. The decision shook him like a thunderbolt. It was obvious that, in spite of everything, he had expected to go free and was struggling to control his emotions when he was led away. A few days later, brought back for sentencing, he looked ashen and could barely control his emotions as the judge passed the death sentence. Arthur Hoyt Day was scheduled to hang on December 18.

The condemned man spent his last night on Earth singing gospel hymns and writing letters to his relatives, maintaining his innocence to the very end. One of the letters written was to his sister, Mary, a long and rambling message that reveals an agonizing bitterness. It read in part:

> Sister Mary, I will drop you a few lines hoping they will find you well and in misery and I hope you can't sleep a wink night nor day till you tell the truth. You know you swore my life away to save your own neck, but may God bless you. You ought to be here instead of me, you liar. I hope you won't have a friend in Rochester. They ought to tar and feather you and ride you out of town on a rail... Well, dear Quigley, I will forgive your lies. I hope God will too, but I don't see how you can have the face to come to God and ask him to forgive you in your sins....Oh, how I wish it had been you instead of her, and when you were not satisfied with her death, but hung me too. Oh you hag, you hag, you hell hound.

But while Arthur continued to assert Mary's guilt, the fact remains it was he who was facing the hangman's noose come morning.

The gallows was set up outside the courthouse on East Street in Welland. Hundreds of people had been trailing into town since the previous day, some even bringing picnics and making a holiday of it, though as it turned out, only 100 or so people could fit in the courtyard, leaving the rest disappointed. As the *Welland Tribune* reported, "about seventy persons witnessed the execution, Niagara Falls town being especially well represented. The wind was raw and whilst waiting the grievesome event many kept warm by vigorous marching and counter marching."

Arthur, smartly dressed as always, with the usual flower in his lapel, was led to the gallows at 7:55 AM. His calm demeanor finally cracked. "As the doomed man caught sight of the gallows and dangling rope he became visibly agitated and a scared, haunted look overspread his usual placid countenance," noted the *Oswego Palladium* for December 18. When Arthur mounted the steps to the scaffold, he found a sea of faces beneath him, each eager to witness justice done.

Once atop the scaffold, he suddenly regained his composure, drawing on hidden reserves of courage. "He bore himself with a swagger and to all outward appearance was the least affected and most jaunty of those assembled," reported the

Auburn Bulletin on December 18. "After calmly surveying the crowd of spectators, which numbered several hundred, he shook hands with the jailor, sheriff and minister and simply said good-bye."

Now his arms and legs were bound and a black hood pulled over his head. The time was 7:57. With the minister reciting the Lord's Prayer, the drop was released. A long sigh escaped the crowd at the thud of the rope, but Arthur's neck was not broken by the fall. Instead, he died a slow and agonizing death by strangulation over a span of 10 minutes. Suddenly, the day did not seem festive after all, and people drifted away without speaking.

The execution was more grisly than most would have liked, but few of the assembled onlookers or the countless thousands who followed the trial in newspapers would have felt justice was miscarried. Hoyt wasn't content to merely abandon his wife, he had to kill her, and was callous enough to lure her to Niagara Falls, a haven of romance and relaxation, to do it. Few had it in their hearts to forgive him for that.

CHAPTER EIGHT

Mysteries of the Falls

CAROLINE GILMAN, THE BOSTON-BORN author and poet, claimed nothing was more enchanting than viewing the awe-inspiring Niagara Falls. "I felt the moral influence of the scene acting on my spiritual nature, and while lingering at the summit, alone, offered a simple and humble prayer," she wrote. "I gave myself up to the overpowering greatness of the scene, and my soul was still."

Although the place has changed since Gilman's visit in the early 19th century, Niagara Falls still possesses a magic that the bright lights and gaudy advertising of the tourist industry cannot dispel. Stand near the falls on a bright summer's day, when a brilliant rainbow spans the gorge and sun reflects off the turbulent water like flakes of silver, and feelings of genuine enchantment wash over you. Return to the same spot in wintertime, when a belligerent wind is whipping the waves into a foamy frenzy and ice hangs like death shrouds from the gorge, and you sense the fearsome power and changeable temperament of the place. In either season, a fantastical aura of mystery and magic hangs heavy over the falls.

It's little wonder then that Niagara Falls has played host to countless legends, myths and tales of the supernatural that stretch back centuries.

Native American tradition says that a mighty god, He-No the Thunderer, and his mistress, the Maid of the Mist, reside in a grotto behind the veil of roaring water. It's said that shamans leave gifts of food and goods for these benevolent spirits on the Three Sisters, a trio of tiny islands located just above the falls. Farther downstream, beneath the roiling anger of the Whirlpool, lurks a monstrous serpent that preys upon hapless victims and poisons the very water.

As you travel away from the river, Native American legend gives way to European tales of the supernatural. Among the most infamous of these traditions centers upon the Houdini Magic Hall of Fame, for decades squeezed between wax museums and one of the premier attractions on Clifton Hill. Some believe the museum was plagued by a curse issued by the famed escape artist himself that led to a string of ill-fortune, culminating in a disastrous fire that destroyed the building.

Add to all this an abundance of ghost stories— the spectral soldiers of Lundy's Lane, still fighting a battle long since over; the beautiful, ethereal woman of Victoria Park Restaurant who interrupts dinners with her sudden manifestations; and the hellish stain of the Screaming Tunnel, where the echoes of a grisly murder are quite literally heard to this day.

Combine these ingredients and you have a potent brew of myth and legend that remains as vibrant today as it was in the past. Perhaps no place known to man is as blessed with magic and mystery as Niagara Falls.

Lelawala, Maiden Behind the Myth

Niagara Falls is recognized as one of the great natural wonders of the world, a place of spellbinding beauty and tempestuous majesty. Millions of tourists visit Niagara every year, making it the most famous waterfall in the world. All come away changed forever; standing next to the falls is an unforgettable, almost magical experience.

Since French explorers first laid eyes on the waterfall in the 17th century, we've viewed Niagara Falls with awe. The roar of the crashing water seems to irresistibly pull people toward it, and it proves difficult to cast off its enchantment. Occultist Aleister Crowley alluded to this power when, after visiting Niagara Falls in 1906, he wrote that "my dearest destiny would be to live and die within them."

Author Harriet Beecher Stowe, a woman far less troubled than Crowley, similarly felt prepared to throw herself into the raging waters. "I felt as if I could have gone over with the waters; it would be so beautiful a death; there would be no fear in it," she later explained. "I felt the rock tremble under me with a sort of joy. I was so maddened that I could have gone too, if it had gone."

One Native American woman, known to us today as the Maid of the Mist, the namesake of the world-famous tourist boats, surely felt the same. Her story is among the most hauntingly beautiful of the numerous legends tied to Niagara Falls, a tale both tragic and romantic.

The falls held special meaning for her people. "Niagara" is derived from "nia-gara," the last remaining word of the Neutral tribe that dwelt in this region until the mid-1600s. In their tongue, the word means "mighty thunderer" or "thunder of water," an apt description of the waterfalls that have made Niagara famous. Native American people regarded the river with reverence. They believed a vast cave was behind the crashing veil of water and within that grotto resided the spirit of Niagara, a god-like being called He-No the Thunderer. He-No was said to be the embodiment of pure power. Anyone who visits the falls can easily see why.

Water plunges over the crest at speeds of up to 20 miles per hour and with such force that, over the centuries, it has worn a plunge pool 172 feet deep below the falls—every second, an incredible 100,000 cubic feet of water thunders over the edge. In the days before Europeans decided to shape the river to their own interests by diverting water for hydroelectric generation, the falls thundered with even greater power—as much as 202,000 cubic feet of water poured over the falls every second, at speeds in excess of 25 miles per hour.

Native Americans took great comfort in the awesome power of the roaring waters; as long as they flowed, they knew He-No was there to answer their prayers. This god cared deeply for his people, blessing them with health and bountiful crops and protecting them from evil spirits such as the Evil One, a gargantuan snake that resided in the waters of the Niagara River. The periodic battles between He-No and his sworn enemy were epic and often caused rocks to crumble from the gorge walls and fall into the river below (a colorful Native American explanation for what was actually the result of the erosion process).

On occasion, He-No also took an active interest in the lives of those who worshipped him, as he did with Lelawala, the woman we know today as the Maid of the Mist. Lelawala was a beautiful Native American woman from the Neutral tribe, a young girl barely in her teens and yet headstrong. She clashed repeatedly with her father, a tribal chief and a conservative man who expected that his word be obeyed and his expectations met unfailingly. Lelawala's most violent quarrels with her father were over her suitors. The chief expected his daughter to marry a man of fine pedigree, someone who would improve the family line.

The young maiden saw things quite differently than did her father, for she knew the power and allure of love. Friendship with a certain Native man had blossomed into love, and it was he whom Lelawala intended to marry. Many times, the young lovers strolled along the banks of the Niagara River and held each other at a special spot overlooking the falls. The fact that the brave was of a minor family and of no particular importance did not concern Lelawala. She knew this was the man she wanted to be with. And so, with the innocence of a young woman in love, she approached her father and asked for his permission to marry him.

Not surprisingly, Lelawala's father refused. What's more, he was furious that she had gone against his wishes. The chief forbade his daughter from ever seeing her beloved again and began hastily preparing for a wedding with a more suitable groom, a man of his own choosing. Lelawala cried and begged her father to relent, for she could never marry another man after she had tasted love. Her father's will was iron, however, and his decision final.

The notion of marrying a man she did not care for caused something to snap within the beautiful young girl. She couldn't bear to live in a loveless union, and, seeing no other way out, she vowed to let death be her escape. When the moon was high in the night sky, Lelawala slipped away from her

longhouse and crept down to the edge of the Niagara River, where she pushed a white birch-bark
canoe into the water. There was little need to
paddle; the pull of the mighty falls took hold of the
canoe and dragged Lelawala to her fate. She com-
forted herself by singing a hauntingly beautiful
death chant, knowing in her heart that she had
made the right decision. To live without her love
would be a life of hollowness and misery. As her
canoe plummeted over the falls, her lover's name
was on her lips.

She was pulled down the 177-foot cliff and was
lost forever within the mist that forms at the base
of the falls. Presumably, Lelawala's canoe crashed
upon the rocks, but her body was never found. Her
spirit was rescued from an eternity of aimless wan-
dering by He-No the Thunderer, who gently caught
her falling body with his powerful arms. The god
was taken aback by her beauty and courage, and
he was moved by sympathy to give the tragic
w   falls. There,
                                                   to
                                            rnal
                                   ver since
                              joy bursting
                        t gives birth to
        infamous rainbow.

the only shadow on Lelawala's happiness was
a continual longing to see her people one final
time, to say goodbye and to let her father know she

had forgiven him so that he would no longer be wracked by guilt.

Her chance came in an unexpected and unwelcome way. One day, the Evil One resurfaced after an absence of many years, emerging from his underwater lair and swimming up the Niagara River to plague Lelawala's people once again. The serpentine beast had not fully recovered from a previous battle with He-No, and its scaled body was covered in festering wounds that seeped evil-tainted blood into the water and left it poisoned. Lelawala's people became sick from drinking the fouled water, and it seemed that every day they buried a new body. Under the cover of darkness, the monstrous snake ventured onto land, unearthed the dead and devoured their corpses. Terror gripped the Neutral tribe.

Fearing for her people, Lelawala begged He-No that she be allowed to return for one hour to warn them of the true nature of the danger they faced. He agreed, lifting her through the falls and carrying her upon the wind to her childhood village. Family and friends were startled to see Lelawala alive, no one more so than her grieving father, who blamed himself for her death and was all but crippled by guilt. They were also startled to hear that the water they drank, the very water they poured through the cracked lips of the fever-stricken, was the cause of the pestilence among them. Lelawala advised her people to move inland, away from the river and to higher country until the danger had passed. By this time, the hour was over. Lelawala embraced her father fiercely one final time, whispering that she loved him and had long since forgiven his stubbornness. At last, after years of suffering, the old chief's heart was no longer heavy with sadness. Then He-No came and took Lelawala back to her home behind the falls.

A few days later, moved by hunger pangs, the Evil One returned to the village in search of a meal. To its surprise, there were no corpses to devour. Hissing in anger, it slithered through the village, intent on taking revenge. When it found the village eerily silent and completely deserted, the serpent flew into a rage. The Evil One wouldn't be so easily deterred, and, instead of returning to its dark hole, it started to follow its prey inland.

When He-No realized the monstrous snake hadn't given up, he knew he had to act to save his worshippers from destruction. He rose up through the mist of the falls to once again confront his age-old adversary in what was to be a battle to the end. He-No threw a great thunderbolt at the creature and killed it in one mighty blast. The snake's giant body rolled back into the Niagara River and floated downstream, eventually coming to rest in a semi-circle just above the cataract. Its weight, bloated from having feasted on so many of the dead village people, was too much for the cliff face to bear.

A mighty rumble erupted, and then much of the rock over which the falls poured gave way, creating the now-distinctive shape of the Horseshoe Falls.

Some legends say He-No's cavern home was destroyed by the collapse, and that he and Lela-wala went up into the sky to make a new home among the clouds. From this place, they watched over their people. Others say that the couple continues to reside in a cave hidden from view by the roaring curtain of water. In either version, He-No's voice is still heard in the thunder of Niagara's waters, and Lelawala continues to form the rainbows eagerly awaited by camera-happy tourists.

Together, He-No and Lelawala, his Maid of the Mist, provide a constant supernatural presence at Niagara Falls. On sunny days, many visitors claim to see the Indian maiden floating in and out of the mists that shroud the base of the falls. Others see her image in the rainbow that arches over the river. Such sightings or visions, call them what you will, supposedly continue to this day.

Tragically, the beauty and wonder of Niagara Falls isn't appreciated by everyone. For some, the "call of the falls" is so overwhelming that they "take the plunge" and commit suicide by throwing themselves on Niagara's mercy. If Native American legend is to be believed, Lelawala meets their spirits within the mists and welcomes them into her refuge behind the falls. They become a part of the

legend of Niagara Falls, taking their place alongside the tragic Maid of the Mist.

Devil's Gorge

People standing on the shores of the mighty
Niagara River have been known to hear whispers
and disembodied voices alongside the roar of the
water, to see mysterious apparitions floating above
the white-capped waves or become unnerved
by an overwhelming sense of being watched by
unseen eyes. Some have even been startled by the
bone-chilling screams of victims who were long
ago claimed by these rapids. Such are common
experiences at the chillingly named Devil's Gorge.

Next to the falls themselves, one of Niagara's
most famous and spectacular natural attractions is
the Lower Great Gorge, located four miles downstream from Niagara Falls. The water froths and
churns violently as it passes through rapids
and then becomes trapped in a whirlpool, racing
by at speeds in excess of 30 feet per second.
Whether experiencing it from the safety of the
shore, from the dizzying heights of the Aero Car or
during an exhilarating whirlpool jet boat tour, this
natural phenomenon is an unforgettable part of
any visit to Niagara. Many consider it a must-see
attraction.

Although most people are familiar with the
stunning, primal fury of the water, there is a darker
side to Lower Great Gorge as well. No other spot
along the Niagara River is known to have had as

many misfortunes and tragedies over the centuries, generating stories of dark curses, malicious spirits of great power and restless ghosts. These unsettling tales of horror and woe have given rise to this stretch of water's more common name: Devil's Gorge.

At only 250 feet wide, Devil's Gorge is the narrowest point in the Niagara River, a place where nearly four million gallons of water per second is suddenly forced into a bottleneck canyon. The result is a violent maelstrom from which few who enter—willingly or otherwise—ever emerge safely. Also contributing to the white-water rapids is the sudden and dramatic descent of the river—an astounding 47 feet in less than one-third of a mile.

To the Native Americans who resided in the area, Devil's Gorge was much more than just a natural wonder. It was also a place infused with great power and spiritual significance. Rather than hold it sacred, as many such spots were, Native Americans shunned the gorge and feared its magic. They believed that the rapid-tossed waters were home to an abomination responsible for unspeakable terrors.

The creature was most defined in the lore of the Iroquois people, among whom it was known as the Evil One. Residing in a lightless cave located on the American side of the gorge, the Evil One ruled the angry depths of the Niagara River. Festering within the watery abyss, the creature resembled a frighteningly huge snake, its coiled black body bloated from feeding on countless human bodies. Often, the Evil One was also depicted as a grotesque freak of nature, with a frothing mouth and devilish eyes set in a wolf-like head.

Such was the vileness of this spirit that over time its presence poisoned the entire gorge with an aura of malediction. This stretch of the Niagara River became cursed, a place where natural disasters, accidents and violence occurred with uncommon frequency. The heart of this dark power was the lair of the Evil One, a cavern that came to be known as Devil's Hole. The Native people of the area knew that to enter this cave was to bring misfortune and ultimately death upon oneself.

French explorer Robert de la Salle was the first recorded individual to run afoul of the curse of Devil's Gorge. He visited the Niagara area around 1678 but unwisely ignored the counsel of his Native American guides and decided to view the natural spectacle of the whirlpool. La Salle was no doubt held breathless at the sight he beheld. A brave and courageous man, he even dared to venture into the cave of the Evil One. La Salle emerged from the darkened depths a while later, unscathed and more contemptuous than ever of Native American superstition.

But the visit came at a high price. La Salle's fortunes took a sudden turn for the worse. Whereas before he led a charmed existence as an explorer, after his visit to the cave he was plagued by mishap and bad luck. In 1687, he was murdered by members of his own expedition while attempting to explore the Mississippi River for the second time. The motive for his killing has never been concretely established, but many Native Americans were quick to blame the Devil's Gorge curse.

A century later, the gorge was the site of an even greater tragedy, and, once again, the darkness surrounding this evil place was said to play a part. In 1763, Pontiac, chief of the Ottawa Indians, launched a war designed to drive American settlers and British soldiers from the lands west of the Appalachian Mountains. Tribes stormed villages and forts in New York State and Virginia, literally setting the frontier ablaze in an inferno of vengeance.

Among these vicious clashes was a particularly bloody engagement that came to be known as the Devil's Hole Massacre. On September 14, 1763, a column of two dozen British soldiers transporting supplies to Fort Niagara was ambushed along the gorge and massacred by Iroquois braves. Only two people escaped. One man was able to flee into the woods and evade his enemies, while a young drummer boy chose to throw himself over the cliff rather than face a tomahawk. He miraculously survived when his suspenders got caught in the branches of a tree. The garrison at nearby Fort Gray heard the fighting and hurried to assist the supply column. They too were ambushed, and all 80 members of the unit were killed, scalped and their bodies mutilated. Horses, looted wagons, corpses and, if legends are to be believed, even some wounded and screaming victims were thrown into the gorge and a nearby stream that became known as Blood Run.

Some suggest Native Americans were driven to such unprecedented viciousness by the evil taint of Devil's Gorge, which fueled their rage for vengeance. Others, however, believe that the grisly scene was a mass sacrifice to the fiendish spirits said to inhabit this stretch of the river, and that perhaps the Iroquois and their allies were even possessed by the Evil One itself and compelled to perform the savage bloodletting. Who can say? Maybe it was actually a measure of both. But what's certain is that the massacre left a haunting residue in Devil's Gorge that has yet to be washed out.

There were still more tragic incidents involving Devil's Gorge. On September 6, 1901, American President William McKinley viewed the whirlpool from the sightseeing Great Gorge Trolley that ran along its banks. He might have been fine had he remained within the trolley. Instead, like La Salle before him, President McKinley was so captivated by the experience and so intrigued by the various legends that he insisted upon entering Devil's Hole. Only five days later, he was assassinated in Buffalo while paying an official visit to the Pan American Exposition.

Worse was to follow. On March 12, 1907, an avalanche of ice killed three people aboard the Great Gorge Trolley as it wound its way around Devil's Gorge. Then, in 1910, two trolleys crashed head-on near the same spot, derailing both cars and leaving two passengers badly injured. Five years later, on July 15, 1915, a heavy, overloaded trolley ran off the tracks and flung dozens of passengers into the white-capped waters. Thirteen drowned in the raging river, and 70 more were injured.

The Evil One claimed more victims on July 1, 1917, when yet another trolley derailed alongside Devil's Gorge. The car rolled end-over-end down a 30-foot embankment and came to rest in the angry river. Estimates of the number of people who died that day range from 12 to more than two dozen; an exact figure of how many people tragically perished is impossible to determine because the fare register was lost in the crash and some bodies were lost forever in the river. The actual death toll for that day is just another of Niagara's mysteries. But regardless of the actual number of casualties, the disaster yet again brought the cursed history of this stretch of the Niagara River to the public's attention.

Sadly, it's said that every year at least one person loses his or her life by falling or jumping off the rocky cliff. True, these deaths might be the result of simple accidents or moments of final despair. Then again, maybe the river itself is calling out to people, luring them to their doom.

With this chain of horrors providing an endless supply of fuel for the imagination, is it any wonder that Devil's Gorge is reputed to be haunted by dozens, if not hundreds, of tortured souls? If even a few of the stories are true, this length of the Niagara River might lay claim to being the most heavily haunted location in all of Canada.

Visitors to Niagara Glen Nature Reserve, a beautiful park-like setting located along the shores of Devil's Gorge, come expecting to get a close-up view of the turbulent waters, to witness the wonder of the gorge from a different perspective and to sense the true power of the Niagara River as it rages past. Yet some get an entirely different experience than that advertised in the tourist brochures.

These unfortunate visitors encounter evidence, in a variety of haunting forms, of spirits that are unable to move on. Whereas some people might sense a creeping hostility that puts their nerves on edge, others might see the hazy form of a long-dead individual, standing motionless along the shore and looking forlornly over the water that is their grave. It's not unusual to hear desperate cries for help without a discernible source or to sense dramatic cold spots that have a way of making people feel unwelcome. All serve as spine-tingling reminders of the hundreds of souls who lost their lives in Devil's Gorge over the centuries.

Although it's easy for many of us today to accept the possibility of ghosts, it's much more difficult to believe in mythological creatures. Like La Salle and McKinley before us, modern people are often dismissive of Native American tales, generally considering them to be little more than colorful folklore. The very idea that a bloodthirsty serpent possessing unspeakable evil powers might inhabit Devil's Gorge surely strikes many as preposterous, nothing more than a fanciful tale or figments of our collective imagination. And yet eyewitnesses from across the Niagara Region occasionally come forward claiming to have seen something eerily similar.

For example, reports of a giant snake residing in the waters of Lakes Ontario and Erie date back hundreds of years. One of the first recorded occurred in 1819, when a man reported seeing a creature that was dark mahogany in color, up to 50 feet in length and four feet in diameter, with a dog-like head and fins. Later, throughout 1871, the creature was spotted numerous times by reputable people in the Welland and Niagara rivers. Even today, new stories emerge every few years of people who have supposedly witnessed a reptilian-like creature in the Niagara River or adjoining bodies of water.

With dozens of eyewitness accounts from around Niagara, all of which seem to support its existence, perhaps the ancient Native American belief in the Evil One is not unwarranted. Maybe something does indeed reside within the depths of Devil's Gorge.

It's even rumored that modern Satan worshippers frequent the area, specifically Devil's Hole cave, in the hopes of tapping into the hellish power infused within. The Satan worshippers' shadowy and secretive rituals are rarely seen or reported, but one hopes their efforts to commune with the Evil One or channel the gorge's vile magic are in vain.

But whether Devil's Gorge is cursed with foul magic, populated by ghostly victims stretching back centuries or home to a bloodthirsty snake of epic proportions, thanks to a long history of tragedy, it more than lives up to its ominous name.

So if you get a chance to visit Devil's Gorge, open yourself up to the secrets of long ago that lie beneath the water. Keep an open mind about the possibilities. And listen closely, because the roar of the river might not be the only sound you hear. You might hear the cries of ghostly victims trapped within the rapids, the whispered lure of the curse as it tempts new victims into the water's deathly embrace or even the hissing bile of the Evil One itself.

Houdini Magic Hall of Fame

The wonders performed by magicians amaze young and old alike, even if we accept that they are merely stagecraft and illusion. There's something timeless about our fascination with magic, just as there seems to be an enduring fascination with the greatest performer of the mystic arts— Harry Houdini.

No doubt, part of his allure is a result of the mysteries that magicians shroud themselves in. They are, after all, a secretive brotherhood. They jealously guard the tricks of their trade, and their secrets seem to live and die with them. Imagine how illusionists would react if their magic paraphernalia was put on display for all to see. They'd probably feel angry and betrayed, perhaps even vengeful. But would this bitterness compel them to find an arcane way to curse the displayed items? And would this resentment even be strong enough to cause a magician to return from beyond the grave in an effort to ensure that his secrets remained a mystery?

Rational minds might dismiss such notions out of hand. And yet, many believe Harry Houdini did both—cast a hex and return from beyond the grave—when his entire collection of stagecraft equipment was turned into feature exhibits at the Houdini Hall of Fame in Niagara Falls, which for many years was one of Clifton Hill's most famed attractions. The evidence seems compelling, but each of us must decide for ourselves what we believe.

Harry Houdini was born Erich Weiss to a poor Jewish family in Budapest, Hungary, on March 24, 1874. He took his immortal stage name in honor of his idol, the French magician Jean Eugene Robert Houdin. In time, however, Harry surpassed the achievements and renown of Houdin, and indeed all other magicians of the day, to become the greatest escape artist and illusionist the world had ever seen.

Houdini's life, like the acts he performed on stage, was full of drama and shrouded in mystery. Some claim, for example, that he was a spy in the employ of Scotland Yard. Others, most notably Sir Arthur Conan Doyle, the creator of Sherlock Holmes and at one point a close friend of Houdini, claimed that Harry was a medium who used supernatural abilities to perform his stunts. Certainly, the magician kept his stunts a closely guarded secret and often outwardly lied about his background to retain an air of the unknown about himself.

If anything though, Houdini's death and afterlife are even more mysterious than the life he led. He died on October 31, 1926, at Grace Hospital in Detroit. Stories that his death was the result of a failed stage act or a punch in the stomach are false; in truth, he died of peritonitis, internal poisoning resulting from a ruptured appendix.

Many people find it oddly appropriate that the world's greatest magician should die on Halloween and that he was 52 years old at the time, the exact number of cards in a deck. Interestingly, Houdini was born 26 years before the turn of the century and died 26 years into the new century, as if his life's deck had been deftly cut in half by fate. Are these oddities surrounding his death a coincidence, or are they evidence that his life was shaped by destiny?

In his last will and testament, Houdini bequeathed his magic paraphernalia to his brother Theodore, who had followed him into the industry and was known professionally as Hardeen. Theodore was free to make use of the items but was left with strict instructions that they be burned upon his retirement, so that no one would discover the secrets of their stagecraft.

For reasons unknown, Theodore did not follow his brother's implicit instructions. Instead, the effects were put into storage and, for a while at least, forgotten. Then, in 1967, the collection of magic items was rediscovered and put up for sale. Houdini must have been rolling over in his grave. The secrets of his life's work would be revealed, and the legacy of mystery and marvel that he had worked so hard to preserve would be dashed.

After learning of the sale from an article appearing in the *Toronto Star*, entrepreneur Henry Muller saw an opportunity to combine the timeless reputation of Houdini with the kitsch of Niagara Falls and make a fortune. Muller envisioned a museum honoring the exploits of the great magician, a place where his legend could be placed in perspective and preserved for future generations.

Certainly there was historic precedence for locating the museum in Niagara Falls, for though Harry Houdini traveled extensively, he was drawn to the power and mystique of the falls. He visited its splendor several times with his beloved wife, Bess, and upon forming the Houdini Picture Corporation in 1919, made sure that the first film created under his label included the falls.

Filming of *The Man From Beyond*, which Harry Houdini not only produced but also starred in, took place at Niagara Falls in May 1921. One of the most celebrated scenes in the movie depicts Houdini swimming through the rapids above the cataract to rescue the heroine from certain death. It was a stunning performance, the equal of any of his stagecraft stunts for sheer drama, and the promotions played it for all it was worth.

SEE him fight to the death on the edge of the rocky cliff 800 feet above the yawning chasm! SEE him make his sensational swim of the rapids of Niagara! SEE him accomplish the unparalleled thrill of all times—the rescue of the girl on the very brink of Niagara Falls itself!

What the audiences didn't realize was that Houdini's audacious "fight to the death on the edge of the rocky cliff" was nothing more than a Hollywood effect; he was in no danger, and the swim through the rapids certainly did not test his physical mettle, because he was strapped into a leather harness that slid on a cable and made the stunt effortless. Still, it was captivating to watch the undisputed master of magic onscreen in a location so shrouded in mystical allure.

Harry Houdini, the world's greatest magician and escape artist, felt an affinity for Niagara Falls. Some say his spirit returned to the falls, specifically to the museum housing his paraphernalia, after his tragic death.

Entrepreneur Henry Muller was banking that this fascination remained even some 40 years after Houdini's untimely death. Muller was certain of success, and his enthusiasm for the project easily won over a group of willing investors. With the money in place, he made a successful bid for the Houdini estate. To house the vast collection, a former meat-packing plant on Centre Street and near Niagara's tourist core at Clifton Hill was purchased and extensively renovated. Then, on June 6, 1968, the doors to the Houdini Magical Hall of Fame were swung open to the eager public.

Muller and his investors were pleased with the reception, but it seems as though a long-dead Houdini was not. He let his displeasure be known early and frequently.

During the first year of the museum's operation, there were a series of six mysterious fires in the building, a robbery and a freak accident in which one of the museum directors walked through a plate glass window and died an excruciating death. This string of inexplicable misfortune caused many to speculate that the museum was cursed, and, if indeed it was, the logical choice for the offending spirit was Harry Houdini himself. For a man who had cheated death so many times and had developed an avowed interest in mysticism, voicing his anger from beyond the grave didn't seem impossible or even extraordinary.

If it was Houdini's intent to deter Muller and his partners, he failed. They weren't put off by the odd happenings, but they soon recognized the necessity of a new facility, one more suited to the museum's needs and even closer to the well-traveled tourist paths of Niagara Falls. In 1972, they purchased the historic 19th-century Victoria Park train station atop Clifton Hill, and the Houdini Magical Hall of Fame made the short move.

Almost as soon as the magic artifacts were placed in their new displays, it became obvious that the curse had followed them. Strange noises were commonplace, and objects moved of their own accord. Staff would open the doors in the morning to find exhibits rearranged or objects toppled over. No logical explanation was ever found. Perplexing phenomena continued until the museum's ultimate demise.

If there was ever any doubt in anyone's mind that Houdini's spirit was behind this mayhem, they were dispelled after a chilling séance held in 1974, when the dead magician definitely let it be known he was present in the museum and not in a good frame of mind.

The séance, as with the many held within the museum before this one, had its roots in the complex set of beliefs that shaped Houdini. Although he may have expended a great deal of energy in exposing fraudulent mystics, Houdini believed strongly in the possibility of communicating with the dead and tried several times to speak with his beloved mother. It was this earnest hope for a legitimate spiritual experience that caused him to hate those who preyed on the grief-stricken by staging false séances.

Even after having exposed dozens of fakes, Houdini still believed...or at least, wanted to believe. He even promised his wife, Bess, that should he die before her (which, in fact, he did) he would try to prove the theory of life-after-death by communicating with her from beyond the grave. The anniversary of his death, October 31, became the commonly accepted date of the communication, and so numerous séances were held on Halloween over the ensuing years. Among those who attended were important figures such as mentalist Joseph Dunniger and author Walter B. Gibson, a magician and author, both close friends of Houdini, as well as magicians such as the Great Randi. None of the early séances met with any success, however, and Houdini never communicated with his wife.

The tradition of annual séances continued when the Houdini Magical Hall of Fame opened. Over the course of the museum's existence, several were held within its blackened, silence-shrouded confines late on the evenings of October 31. Despite the excitement they generated, none of these séances resulted in anything of real consequence, certainly nothing that convinced the participants of the existence of ghosts. Then came the séance of 1974, and everything changed.

Medium Ann Fisher explained to Houdini that this might well be the last séance held in his honor unless he made his presence known. He had to provide a sign of some kind to justify the annual gatherings. For long, breathless seconds, nothing happened. And then—crash! Chairs suddenly emptied as everyone jumped to their feet. At their feet, lying in shards, its earth spilling out onto the floor, was a flower pot that just moments earlier had stood securely on a bookshelf containing volumes about Houdini's life.

But there was more. Next to the shattered pot was a book that had fallen open to a page featuring a Houdini poster that boldly asked "DO SPIRITS RETURN?" The answer to that question, at least as far as those who had gathered together that Halloween evening were concerned, was a resounding yes. Houdini had kept his promise. He returned from the grave to prove that there is life, or some form of personal survival, after death.

Several subsequent séances also met with success, with mediums claiming to have seen and spoken to the spirit of the great magician. Through these mediums, Houdini expressed growing displeasure that his wishes regarding his magic paraphernalia were ignored. His spirit insisted the items should be destroyed, as his will had dictated.

The museum owners ignored these warnings at their own peril.

On the night of April 30, 1995, a fire started in the Houdini Magic Hall of Fame. The flames took hold and immediately began racing through the exhibit halls, spreading so fast that responding firefighters were powerless to stop their relentless advance. By morning, the building had been gutted and most of its contents destroyed in the spectacular blaze. It seemed that Houdini's wishes had finally been carried out. The cause of the fire has never been determined, causing some to even blame the deceased magician himself.

Today, the Ripley's Four Dimensional Movie Theatre stands on the grounds of the former museum, and Niagara Falls' troubled connection with Houdini has been largely forgotten. The curtains have drawn on Harry Houdini, the man who blurred the line between magic and mysticism.

Or have they? Though he may no longer perform poltergeist performances in Niagara Falls, it's believed that Harry Houdini still takes to the stage at his former homes. Both his New York and Los Angeles mansions are said to be frequented by his shadowy apparition. The New York home still stands, its owners through the years often complaining of mysterious happenings and ghostly visitations. Even though Houdini's Los Angeles house was burned to the ground in 1959, his ghost is reported to still appear among its melancholy ruins.

It was said that while he lived, there was not a form of confinement from which Harry Houdini could not escape. Perhaps the master magician can no more be bound by the shackles of death than he could by straightjackets or handcuffs in life.

CHAPTER NINE

Highlights in History

FOR A RELATIVELY SMALL city, Niagara Falls has experienced a great many things of national or even international importance. Similarly, several people of wide renown made their mark upon its history. Some of these people and events stepped onto the stage for only a brief moment; others continue to reverberate to this day. It's almost as if the community, at the crossroads between Canada and the United States, is also located at the crossroads of history.

During the War of 1812, some of the largest and most critical battles fought on Canadian soil occurred here—the Battle of Lundy's Lane, the Battle of Chippawa and the Battle of Queenston Heights. On a more peaceful front, on February 25, 1878, the world's first international telephone hook-up took place between Niagara Falls and New York City. The first photographs in Canada, daguerreotypes shot by Hugh Pattinson, were taken in Niagara Falls in 1840. And, in the years before the emancipation of slaves, the city served as an end-point for the Underground Railway, by which escaped slaves fled to safety in Canada.

Various luminaries blessed this community with their presence over the years. Sir Harry Oakes, one of the wealthiest men in Canada at one time, left his legacy in Niagara in the form of Oakes Garden Theatre and Oak Hall. He was murdered under mysterious circumstances in 1943. Others include John Fanning, Ontario's first stagecoach operator; Thomas Barnett, who founded one of the first museums in North America, containing an eclectic collection accumulated during his world travels; and James Lewis Kraft, who first patented a method of processing cheese and founded the Kraft Company, was born and raised in a nearby hamlet.

In this chapter, we focus on three of the landmark events and people in Niagara's history: the day the Niagara River actually ran dry; the West's most feared gunslinger, Wild Bill Hickok, who came to the community and laid the foundations for Buffalo Bill Cody's world-famous Wild West show; and the work of brilliant but unheralded inventor Nikola Tesla, which made it possible to harness Niagara's power for electricity.

The Day the Niagara River Ran Dry

Could you ever imagine a day when the great Niagara River would stop flowing, or that a resident of the community could wake up one morning and not hear the roaring thunder of the ever-flowing water? It sounds preposterous, and yet it happened. For almost two whole days back in 1848, Niagara Falls ran dry.

How is it possible that a waterfall over which 100,000 cubic feet of water flows every second could suddenly dry up? What mysterious circumstances led to this freak of nature, a one-time historical event that seems almost impossible to people today? A century and a half later, the day the Niagara River ran dry remains one of the most dramatic events associated with the area.

The exact time the falls went barren was not specifically recorded—news reports in the mid-19th century were sketchy at best—but it's believed to have occurred near midnight on March 29. One of the first people to be alerted to the unique phenomenon was Thomas Street. Around 5:00 AM, he was awakened from a sound sleep by a loud and urgent knocking on his front door. Startled and in a haze, Street tried not to stumble as he ran down the stairs to see whoever might be at his door at such a ghastly hour. His steps were hastened by the desperation in the rapping and a realization that for someone to be at his home at such an unusual hour, the matter must be important indeed.

Thomas Street was one of the wealthiest men in town, owning and operating the large Bridgewater Mills complex, consisting of both grist and sawmills. These water-powered industries employed many men in Niagara Falls and brought with them considerable stature and influence. As he made his way downstairs, possible reasons for the urgent summons raced through Street's mind; for a man of his importance, the possibilities were endless. But Street simply could not have imagined the true nature of the early-morning summons.

The knocking grew more urgent, and Street hastened his stride. When he pulled open the door, he was greeted by his long-time miller who, breathless and excited, tried desperately to get words out. Finally, he managed to tell Street that the mills had stopped working. They had simply ground to a halt. When he had investigated the cause, the miller was shocked to find not only the millrace empty of water but also the whole Niagara River.

Street was dumbfounded by the news. Impossible! The Niagara could not possibly be dry. He hurriedly dressed and decided to see for himself. Thomas Street lived in a large home known as Clark Hill, which stood just above what are now known as the Dufferin Islands. His mills were located just below his house and alongside the rapids, roughly where the Toronto Powerhouse now stands. It was therefore just a short run down the embankment to the river's edge. When he arrived, Street stood in stunned amazement and began to rub his eyes. He couldn't believe what lay before him. "I saw the river channel, on whose banks I had been born 34 years previous almost entirely dry," he wrote later.

By now, other residents along the Niagara River were waking to an eerie silence and the realization that something was abnormal. The ever-present roar of the falls was absent. One by one, they began to gather along the river to see what could have caused this occurrence, finding to their horror, as Thomas Street already had, that the Niagara River was reduced to a mere trickle. By mid-morning, more than 5000 people crowded the banks of the Niagara. The river bed was quickly drying, fish and turtles were left floundering and fighting for their lives on what was now dry land. The mills and factories that were dependent on water power were silent; without their source of power, they were helpless. The once beautiful Niagara River was just a deep gash in the landscape.

Seeing the Niagara all but devoid of water was a shocking, almost frightening, event for most onlookers. And yet, some residents took the opportunity to explore the falls in a way never before—and never since—experienced. Thomas Street was among them. Along with his youngest daughter and a sister who was visiting at the time, he set out to investigate this extraordinary event more carefully. Together, the three walked out to Table Rock, where Street's daughter attached a handkerchief to a walking stick and cheerfully planted it as an impromptu flag, like an explorer of old claiming ownership over a new territory.

They then walked out along the edge of the falls and went one-third of the way across, stopping at Goat Island, which separates Horseshoe Falls from American Falls. They stood on the very brink of the falls and peered into the gorge below, where jagged rocks and massive boulders that were normally obscured by water and mist lay exposed 2200 feet beneath them. Street's face drained of color, and he shuddered at the thought of having frequently passed over these frightening hazards while a passenger aboard the *Maid of the Mist*.

Other spectators had similar ideas, eagerly walking out into the river bed, which only hours before had been a torrent of rapids that would have surely swept anyone to a disastrous death. Some joined the Streets atop the falls, while others ventured into the rubble-strewn river bed below, taking the opportunity to stand at the base of the cliff face and look upward to gain a true appreciation of the height and grandeur of Niagara Falls.

Soon, this incredible act of nature had become a tourist attraction and a media event. People arrived on horseback and by horse and buggy from numerous inland communities, many bringing picnic lunches that they enjoyed on blankets spread out on the dry river bed. Newspaper correspondents from local papers raced to the scene to record the sights and sounds.

One intriguing account appeared in the *Buffalo Express* a few days later, reporting that "all the people in the neighborhood were abroad, exploring recesses and cavities that had never before been explored to mortal eyes." This account seems to suggest that caves might be behind the falls that millions of visitors every year are completely unaware of, caves no one is likely to ever have the chance to view again.

All along the Niagara's length, articles that had been laying at the river's bottom and were hidden for years, in some cases hundreds of years, were now visible to the naked eye. The temptation was too great, and souvenir hunters eagerly ventured out onto the river bed to collect the relics. The most common items retrieved were from the War of 1812, including bayonets, muskets, barrels, cannons and tomahawks.

Thomas Street was one of those who gained a treasure trove of historical artifacts by scavenging from the river bottom. In the early afternoon, after having spent the morning exploring the falls, Street took his sister for a carriage ride along the river to the village of Chippawa. During the excursion, they too noticed the rusty muskets and bayonets lying among the bare rocks at the bottom of the now-dry river. Street decided they must have been thrown into the river by fleeing American soldiers in the aftermath of their decisive defeat at the Battle of Lundy's Lane as they desperately raced for the safety of their encampment at Chippawa. Like many others, Street took the time to collect a few souvenirs as reminder of the momentous day.

Others took advantage of the receding waters in different ways. Below the falls, workers from the *Maid of the Mist* excursion boat were able to venture out onto the river bed and blast away rocks that had been a navigation hazard since tours began in 1846. It was an opportunity that might never again present itself, so they were determined to make the most of it. Meanwhile, a squad of soldiers from the U.S. cavalry rode conducted maneuvers on the river bed, riding up and down its length in exhibition.

Although most people were awed by this unique historical event, many others were terrified by the significance of a river that suddenly and mysteriously dried up. Some came to believe it was the beginning of the apocalypse, a prelude to the end of the world. It occurred to them that this unnatural occurrence might be the harbinger of worst disasters to come.

On the morning of March 30, with the falls still silent, thousands of people on both sides of the border attended special church services. Unsure of what was happening, they turned to their faith to see them through the troubling times. With each passing hour, the level of fear and anxiety among residents grew more intense, spreading like wildfire through communities lining the shores of the Niagara.

Bishop Thomas Brock Fuller, the first Bishop of Niagara and Thomas Street's brother-in-law, took note of the tension in the air and believed the drying up of the Niagara was a warning from God against spiritual weakness. "Even the Indians, then around here," Bishop Fuller remembered

45 years later, "shared in the superstition that something terrible was about to happen and this remarkable freak of the great river was a warning to desist from wickedness." Many agreed and made solemn promises to become more observant of religion thereafter.

Suddenly, it seemed as if the collective prayers had been answered. During the evening, a gathering roar could be heard coming from the direction of Lake Erie, and the ground shook underfoot. Like a tidal wave, a wall of water came thundering down the Niagara River channel and over the edge. The familiar and comforting sound of the falls was heard once again. The return of the water reassured residents that everything was going to be all right, and they collectively breathed a sigh of relief. Thomas Street was among them; the return of the water meant his mills would soon resume operating.

Life went back to normal, and the residents of Niagara Falls soon found out the cause of the remarkable incident that had seen the river run dry. There was nothing apocalyptic or supernatural about it. Instead, it was simply a freak of nature. Severe winter weather, Niagara residents later learned, had created a heavy amount of pack ice (three feet deep in some areas) across Lake Erie, which, as a result of an unusual and prolonged warm spell, had begun to break up by late March. Easterly winds had driven the ice up the lake, but during the early-morning hours of March 29, the winds reversed, sending the ice field in the opposite direction and jamming the entrance of the Niagara River between Buffalo and Fort Erie.

There was so much ice that the river could not possibly handle it all, and, as a result, the flows began to pile up at the entrance. Within a matter of hours, the jam became dense with hundreds of thousands of tons of ice pressing in upon itself and became an impenetrable dam through which almost no water could pass. The river went dry, as if its taps were turned off. Only when the wind shifted again about 40 hours later did the ice dam finally break up, releasing the water and returning the Niagara to its natural state.

So far as is known, nature had never created such a phenomenon at Niagara before, nor has it since. Today, one can only wonder what it must have been like to explore under the raging, mighty Niagara Falls. Unfortunately, because this was a time before the widespread availability of cameras, no photographs could reveal what that eerily unnatural scene must have looked like. We can only see it in our mind's eye.

Wild Bill Hickok

The crowd leaned forward on their bleachers, straining to see the deadliest pistoleer in the Wild West. He certainly cut an impressive figure, standing an athletic 6 feet 2 inches tall, with a long, trailing moustache and flowing, shoulder-length golden hair. He wore a stylish jacket with cutaway swallow tails and wide lapels, the height of fashion, and his face was shaded by a wide-brimmed sombrero. Women in the crowd swooned, and even the men had to admit there was a self-assured, steel-nerved, larger-than-life aura about the man.

He was a living legend: Wild Bill Hickok, frontier scout, gunfighter and lawman. And to the excitement of the gathered crowd, he was in Niagara Falls, hosting and starring in "The Grand Buffalo Hunt," a show described as a thrilling recreation of the Wild West.

The show was the brainchild of Thomas Barnett, a Niagara Falls entrepreneur. Barnett was a native of England who had traveled extensively as a young man and, during his journeys to various exotic locales, had collected a trove of curios and oddities. He finally settled in Niagara Falls, and in 1827 he opened a museum in a small stone building to display his hoard of souvenirs and treasures. An expansion came 10 years later. Then, in 1858, Barnett replaced the aging structure with a large cut-stone building that cost a near-astronomical $140,000.

Sometime in the late 1860s, Barnett began to envision his greatest spectacle yet: a Wild West show with live animals and frontier personalities. People in the cities of eastern Canada were enthralled with all things related to life in the prairies. They read dime novels romanticizing the exploits of outlaws, snapped up newspapers that followed the Indian Wars and dreamt of experiencing the freedom associated with life on the fringes of civilization. In light of this fascination, Barnett was convinced that a show bringing the West to life for eastern viewers would be a resounding success.

Planning for the show began tentatively in 1869, with Barnett's son, Sidney, making a trip to the United States to begin exploring options. Sidney made the acquaintance of William F. "Buffalo Bill" Cody, a frontier scout and future showman, who referred Sidney to John B. "Texas Jack" Omohundro. Cody assured Sidney that Omohundro could help acquire the wild buffalo that would be the centerpiece of the Western show. Barnett also tried to secure the services of Major Frank North, whose Pawnee scouts were famous on the frontier.

Progress was painfully slow, and there were a number of frustrations and delays in organizing what was billed as a "thrilling spectacle." For a time, Barnett began to despair that the show would remain nothing more than a dream, but things came together in 1872.

Sidney Barnett traveled to Fort McPherson in May to further the plans. On June 12, the *Omaha Weekly Herald* published a letter from a correspondent at Fort McPherson dated June 3. "A novel undertaking is on foot here, and is of gigantic proportions," the correspondent reported. "Colonel Sidney Barnett, of Niagara Falls, is getting up a grand

Buffalo hunt at Niagara Falls, from the 1st to the 4th of July. He is now here for the purpose of completing arrangements and superintending the starting of the enterprise, and shipping the buffaloes East.

"He has secured the services of the celebrated scout and hunter, Mr. J.B. Omohundro, better known as 'Texas Jack,' the hero of the Loup Fork," the letter continued. "'Texas Jack' is a partner of 'Buffalo Bill,' and nothing that skill and foresight can accomplish will be spared to make this hunt a perfect success. Through the kindness of Major North, the commander of the Pawnee scouts, arrangements are being made for a party of Pawnee Indians...to go to Niagara with their fleet ponies and lodges, and full war and hunting equipment. The buffaloes will pass through Omaha the latter part of this, or early part of next month."

Things were certainly looking good, and the Barnetts were elated. Unfortunately, it was all a cruel illusion.

No sooner had the ink dried on the newspaper than problems began to emerge. The United States government, through their Indian agent, refused to grant the Pawnee permission to participate. Then Omohundro backed out suddenly, and most of the captured buffalo died. This meant that Barnett had no events for his show and not enough time to make alternate arrangements before the planned Fourth of July show date. Despondent, but not yet willing to give up on his dream, Barnett announced a postponement until August.

Sidney Barnett raced across the breadth and width of the West, desperately seeking acts for the show. He hired some Sac and Fox Indians, and a few Mexican cowboys, and obtained a fresh lot of buffalo. Most impressively, he managed to secure the services of Wild Bill Hickok, one of the most daring and dashing scouts in the West, to star in and direct the event.

Hickok, already a legend in his own time, was a true son of the West. He was born James Butler Hickok in Troy Grove, Illinois, in 1837, and by the time he was a teenager was considered the best shot in the state and handy in a brawl. At the age of only 20, he was named constable of Monticello Township, in Kansas, beginning an on-again off-again career as a lawman. Hickok later served as a scout during the Civil War but earned his notoriety as a dead-shot and proficient man-killer during postwar stints as a drifting gambler, scout and courier for the army and peacekeeper in various rowdy frontier towns.

By 1872, Hickok had been involved in six gunfights, though widely believed fictitious accounts said he had personally killed hundreds of men. His legend had spread across the continent. But he was not a heartless killer, and his reputation as the best pistoleer on the plains weighed heavily on his broad shoulders. Less than a year earlier, he had accidentally killed a friend in a shoot-out, and the guilt weighed heavily on him. It's likely he took Barnett's offer to travel to Niagara Falls as a way of distancing himself from the violence of the cattle towns he frequented.

While Hickok wanted nothing more to do with accolades related to gunfighting, the general public lapped it up, and the people of Niagara Falls eagerly awaited the arrival of this larger-than-life Western hero. During August, posters appeared in the Niagara area advertising what was described as a "Grand Buffalo Hunt" that was to take place in Niagara Falls on the 28th and 30th of that month. The posters went on to say, "this novel and most exciting affair will be under the direction and management of the most celebrated scout and hunter of the great plains, Mr. William Hickok, better known as Wild Bill." Barnett intended to milk every ounce of publicity from his star attraction.

The Grand Buffalo Hunt was staged just above the falls on a 15-acre site that had at one time been used for a racetrack. A plank fence about eight feet high enclosed the arena. Approximately 2000 spectators, who were charged an admission fee of 50 cents per person, sat on bleachers erected at the northwest end of the compound.

The show got underway at 3:00 PM with a lacrosse match featuring Native Canadians from the Grand River Reservation near Kitchener, Ontario. Next, a group of mounted hunters appeared, including the eagerly awaited Wild Bill Hickok, four Native Americans, and four Mexicans who wore large sombreros, black velvet jackets and yellow pants. They all rode up to a pen in the center of the enclosure, where two buffalo and a Texas longhorn ox stood. Though Hickok and his performers tried to put on a good show for the viewers, the animals were less inclined. In fact, they showed little interest in anything other than grazing.

"The first game struck was a Texas ox, but he was not taking a lively interest in the affair and was soon turned out to grass," wrote one journalist. A buffalo cow was then brought out but she, like the longhorn before her, didn't seem inclined to provide the "thrilling spectacle" Barnett had promised. She laid down in the grass, lazing in the sun, and had to be coaxed to even rise to her feet. She stood there, unmoving and unconcerned, as the Mexican cowboys took turns lassoing her.

Next, a "rather mangy looking" bull buffalo was ushered out of the pen. He was in no hurry, strolling "as leisurely as a deacon from church." The animal was eventually prodded into half-heartedly running around the pen while the Native Americans gave chase, but the bull ran so slowly that they often passed it. The only moment of drama came when Hickok tried to rope and capture the bull from horseback. Hickok succeeded in lassoing the buffalo, but the rope, rather than tightening around its neck, slipped over the animal's hump. This gave all the advantage to the buffalo, so when it bolted, it caused Hickok's horse to flip, head over heals. Hickok, the greatest gunfighter in the West, was thrown face first into the dirt and watched as his horse was dragged away by the 1000-pound buffalo.

It wasn't long after this that the bull became bored of the whole affair and stopped to graze. With that, the show was over. Most witnesses left their seats deeply disappointed in the performance, feeling like, as one reporter described, it had been a "swindle" and a "farce." A second showing, two days later, was hardly more entertaining. Thomas Barnett's reputation was tarnished, and he lost heavily on the event, needing to fill the seats with spectators to break even. The debt he incurred caused him, after continued financial reverses, to sell his beloved museum five years later.

The Grand Buffalo Hunt was a disappointment and embarrassment to Hickok as well, but he wasn't ready to give up on showbiz yet. The very next year, he joined Buffalo Bill Cody and a troupe of actors in a stage performance that drew massive crowds if not rave reviews. Hickok, however, was a poor actor who often forgot his lines and never seemed comfortable with all the "make-believe." After a single season on the stage, Hickok tired of all the theater and left for the West he so loved. He never returned to Niagara and was gunned down by a drifter named Jack McCall, shot in the back of the head while playing poker, on August 2, 1876.

Thomas Barnett's much anticipated "thrilling spectacle" was anything but, and it left a sour taste in the mouths of almost all involved, participant and spectator alike. Nevertheless, despite the unsatisfying entertainment and the financial ruin, the show created the formula for Western shows to follow and was perfected by Buffalo Bill Cody a decade later, when he provided the public with a live-action event, complete with cowboys, Indians, buffalo and appearances by Western heroes. In fact, it's possible—indeed, many believe likely—that Hickok shared his experiences at Niagara Falls in 1872 with Cody and thereby planted the seeds that eventually germinated into Buffalo Bill's Wild West.

If this is true, and Thomas Barnett's 1872 production served as the inspiration for Cody's long-running show, then perhaps the "Grand Buffalo Hunt" wasn't a failure after all?

Nikola Tesla

Nikola Tesla was one of history's most brilliant and eccentric minds, and, though he only ever visited Niagara Falls once, he was an important figure in the area's history. A plaque dedicated to Tesla is in Queen Victoria Park, a nine-foot statue stands on Goat Island and within the lobby of Fallsview Casino Resort is a beautiful monument that serves as a tribute to his scientific genius. And yet, few people know it was Nikola Tesla who made it possible to harness the power of Niagara Falls to provide electricity for tens of millions across

Nikola Tesla was one of the most brilliant minds the world has ever known, and yet he's little remembered today. This beautiful monument, located at the entrance of Fallsview Casino Resort, serves to remind us of his role in making hydroelectricity a reality.

Ontario and the eastern United States, revolution-izing life as we know it.

Nikola Tesla was born in the village of Smiljan, then part of the Austro-Hungarian Empire, at mid-night between July 9 and 10, 1856. Though a sickly child, he was unnaturally energetic (requiring no more than two or three hours sleep per night) and very intelligent. When he was a youngster, he could solve difficult mathematical problems almost instantly and without paper, and a photographic memory allowed him to master large volumes of information quickly and with little effort.

When he was in primary school, an event occurred that seemed to foreshadow one of Tesla's crowning moments. Leafing though an old book one day, he came across an image of Niagara Falls. It captured his imagination. As Tesla stared at the picture, he envisioned how the tremendous and unrelenting force of the flowing water could be used to turn a great wheel to create power, much like gristmills along the river had been doing for decades but on a much grander scale and capable of running entire communities. Shortly after this revelation, he told an uncle that he would one day go to America and harness the power of the falls. His amused uncle couldn't have known the youngster would be true to his word.

Tesla's father was less amused by his son's day-dreaming. A Greek Orthodox priest, he had assumed his son would follow him into the clergy and was disappointed when he opted for a life devoted to science instead of God. At the age of 19, Tesla entered the Technical University at Graz, Austria, to study electrical engineering, and he began to think about the possibility of developing a substitute for direct current. He realized that direct current had limited use—it only had a range of about one square mile from the point of generation, and the electricity had to be used as it was manufactured. Tesla became convinced that an alternating current motor that would alleviate these drawbacks was possible, but no one in the academic or scientific community believed him.

Several years later, he had a sudden flash of insight that revealed exactly how the motor should be constructed. He built a prototype, the world's first AC induction motor, which worked perfectly. Still, he could not get anyone interested in his technology. The conservative scientists and leaders of Europe continued to put their faith in direct current and ridiculed Nikola. As a result, he decided to try his luck in the United States, arriving in 1884 with only four cents in his pocket and a letter of introduction to Thomas Edison from one of the famous inventor's European associates, who had met Tesla and recognized his genius.

Edison hired the young engineer to work for him, but Tesla left less than a year later because Edison believed alternating energy was impractical. Edison had a vested interest in discrediting the new technology, because his company had invested heavily in direct current and stood to lose a fortune if alternating energy was adopted.

Tesla's fortunes hit rock bottom. Indeed, at one point, he was reduced to digging ditches and performing other menial tasks to earn a meager wage. Many thought him insane, or at least close to it. When he went for a walk, he always counted every step taken; when he sat down for a meal, he calculated the cubic contents of the plate set before him and wiped the cutlery with 18 linen napkins. The mere sight of a pearl threw him into a fit; looking at a peach was enough to cause him to break into a fever; he had no interest in even the most beautiful of women; and at times, he felt that the very air around him was on fire, causing him great distress, even pain. Tesla's quirks made it difficult for others to take him and his revolutionary theories seriously.

Then, in 1887, his luck suddenly and dramatically changed. Two wealthy backers stepped forward to finance his work, and within a matter of months, the Tesla Electric Company was formed. The machinery necessary to manufacture alternating current was built, and patents were taken out for all aspects of the system. Another stroke of luck came when a prominent inventor, George Westinghouse, probably the most famous scientist in America after Thomas Edison, became an enthusiastic convert to alternating current electricity. Westinghouse purchased Tesla's patents for $1 million plus royalties and hired the engineer to work for him.

In 1893, Tesla demonstrated the alternating current to the public for the first time at the World's Exposition in Chicago. The showman-like scientist thrilled his audience by receiving through his body currents of 200,000 volts, causing his clothing to emit halos of light. He promised an exciting electric future. Niagara Falls, he foretold, had enough horsepower to "light every lamp, drive every railroad, propel every ship, heat every stove and produce every article manufactured by machinery in the United States." It was a bit of an exaggeration, but the point was well taken, and people were sold on alternating current electricity. Instantly, direct current became obsolete, yesterday's technology.

Edison, who had invested a good deal of time and money in the development of direct current, refused to accept defeat in the "war of currents" and mounted a scare campaign designed to give the impression that alternating energy was dangerous. He paid schoolboys 25 cents apiece for stray cats and dogs, which he would electrocute with alternating current before an audience of horrified reporters. Witness the danger of alternating current, Edison would say. Edison even persuaded the warden of Sing Sing prison to electrocute a condemned man using alternating current to demonstrate its lethality. Unfortunately, the charge that had killed the cats and dogs was too weak to kill a man; the prisoner survived, though in great agony, and had to be electrocuted a second time to complete the task.

But Edison's campaign of slander and misinformation failed to dissuade the public. Alternating current went ahead. In 1893, just months after the Chicago Exposition, the Niagara Falls Power Company awarded the Westinghouse Corporation the contract to build the generators for a massive hydroelectric project already underway in Niagara Falls, New York. Tesla's childhood dream of harnessing the power of Niagara Falls was about to become a reality. He had made good on his promise to his uncle.

It was during this time that the scientist made his one and only visit to Niagara Falls. In the summer of 1896, Tesla arrived at the falls, accompanied by Westinghouse, to oversee the progress on the hydroelectric plants. Even at this late stage, there were some concerns about the process working as advertised. Tesla was confident, however, and all doubts were dismissed by the time the hydro plant came online on November 15, 1896. That night, Buffalo began to receive electricity from the generating plant in Niagara Falls, New York, 21 miles away. Never before had electricity on such a large scale been transmitted such a distance; it represented a personal victory for Tesla over his many naysayers and a giant leap forward for society.

It also meant a great deal to Niagara Falls, Ontario. Indeed, Niagara Falls owes more to Tesla than to any other scientist, perhaps any other man. Starting in the early years of the 20th century, hydroelectric generating plants were built on the Canadian side of the Niagara River, all of them using Tesla's alternating current. Within a single decade, Niagara Falls had gone from a town whose economy rested almost solely on tourism to an industrial community central to Ontario's economy. The generating plants encouraged industry to locate there, supplied most of southern Ontario's power needs and helped break the province's crippling dependence on American coal (a strike by Pennsylvania coal workers in 1902 demonstrated the threat posed by reliance on America coal—factories closed, hundreds lost their jobs, and, as winter approached, people shivered in their unheated homes). Tesla's invention allowed Niagara Falls to prosper.

For the next few years, Tesla was the toast of New York and the world, as he made one amazing invention after another. He lectured in America and Europe, giving demonstrations that mystified both scientists and the public. At times, he seemed more like a flamboyant stage magician than a scientist. Throughout the 1890s, he was the most celebrated inventor in the world. But the adulation and success didn't last long, and the latter part of his life was filled with misery and mystery.

The tragic turn in Tesla's fortunes began when a fire swept through the laboratory into which all the money from his patents had been invested. The destruction was complete, wiping out the facilities, his research notes and works in various stages of completion. Because the lab was uninsured, Tesla was financially devastated and never really recovered. Rumors circulated that the fire had been deliberately set, perhaps by a rival who had invested heavily in direct current and had been ruined when Tesla's alternating current swept the world by storm. Whether there is any truth to such innuendo is impossible to determine more than a century later.

Thereafter, Tesla was forced to work with much smaller budgets, often in the form of donations from wealthy patrons. And, though he continued to show off new inventions, none produced patents that businessmen were interested in buying. Consequently, his reputation declined, eclipsed by other inventors and smeared by rivals. He became a recluse, ignored by society, all but forgotten when he died in 1943.

What had Tesla been working on during the final decades of his life? No one knows, but there is a lot of wild speculation. Some suggest he had perfected radar well before it finally emerged in the late 1930s and that he had explored the concept of fluorescent lighting. One unusual claim is that he accidentally caused the Tunguska blast in 1908 during an experiment, perhaps one involving nuclear technology. This is clearly outlandish stuff, yet many of Tesla's papers were seized by the U.S. Defense Department and remain a closely guarded secret. What do they contain that needs to be suppressed more than 65 years later?

Even the circumstances surrounding Tesla's death are wrapped in layers of mystery. He died in his hotel room on January 7, 1943, but it's suggested that he might have been interrogated by government officials in that very room during the three days leading up to this death. It's also whispered among conspiracy theorists that Tesla had been murdered by shadowy members of the government establishment. What is known without a doubt is that, immediately after his death, agents swept down on his hotel room and seized his papers. A few days later, his body was cremated.

It's perhaps fitting that a man who existed on the razor-thin line between genius and madness should die under mysterious circumstances. But Tesla's unusual behavior undermined his legacy. Here was a man who made the transmission of Niagara Falls' power a reality and thus created the industrial heartland of southern Ontario, a man who must surely be ranked among the most brilliant inventors of all time, and yet only six decades after his death, he has become an obscure historical figure.

Whereas Thomas Edison is a household name to this day, Nikola Tesla is hardly known outside the scientific community. It seems his detractors won the final battle—that for fame—in the "war of the currents."

See for Yourself

This book is intended to be entertaining and informative, ideal for a leisurely read while sitting in a comfortable chair. Yet, we also want people to get up off the couch and experience history first-hand. Words on a page cannot do credit to the sites described in the stories in this collection. How do you accurately relate the roar of the falls or the fearsome anger of the Whirlpool Rapids? You can't; you have to see it for yourself. Likewise, there is undoubtedly a thrill in exploring a place in person, and we want to encourage that. After all, part of the concept behind this book is to provide new insight into Niagara's attractions.

We want readers to come to Niagara, to visit some of the places where the dramas we related in this book unfolded and to share some of the appreciation for this remarkable region. To that end, we've provided some information about the more important, publicly accessible locations mentioned in these stories.

Fallsview Casino Resort

The first thing you encounter when passing through the main entrance of this luxurious resort is a unique sculpture, reminiscent of some mad scientist's infernal machine and yet hauntingly beautiful with its dancing lights. The sculpture, known as the Hydro-Teslatron, pays homage to Nikola Tesla, who brought about an electrical revolution. The Fallsview Casino Resort occupies land

Niagara Falls is today known not just for the spectacular falls but also for exciting attractions and luxurious accommodations. Fallsview Casino Resort offers the best of all three.

~o)(o~

that housed one of the earliest hydroelectric distribution stations in Niagara (some of the walls are incorporated in the current structure). But the resort contains more than just a sculpture; there's a beautiful 368-room hotel with a full-service spa, the intimate 1500-seat Avalon Theatre, a shopping galleria with stunning architecture and a wide assortment of shops and restaurants, and of course, the 200,000-square-foot casino, with 150 gaming tables and 3000 slot machines.

Location: 6380 Fallsview Blvd.
www.fallsviewcasinoresort.com

IMAX Theatre

The film *Niagara: Miracles, Myths and Magic* offers viewers a new appreciation for the drama that has unfolded at Niagara Falls over the past few centuries. The re-creation of such important events as the Great Blondin's tightrope antics over the gorge and Annie Taylor's plunge over the falls in a barrel makes for enthralling viewing and brings you closer to the stories than any book ever could.

Also located within the theatre is the Niagara Falls Daredevil Gallery, which includes an impressive collection of original daredevil paraphernalia (including several barrels).

Location: 6170 Fallsview Blvd.
http://www.imax niagara.com/

Maid of the Mist

A trip to the falls would not be complete without an excursion aboard the *Maid of the Mist*. It's the best way to get an appreciation for the sheer size and awesome power of the waterfall. Looking up from the deck of the little tour boats, the thundering sheet of water seems impossibly high and the roar almost deafening in its intensity. Though you'll be provided with a rain poncho, be prepared to get wet nonetheless.

Location: 5920 River Road
www.maidofthemist.com

Niagara Glen Nature Preserve

Here, visitors descend a staircase 200 feet into the gorge, where a series of seven short, interconnected pathways totaling 2½ miles lead through the nature preserve and past a variety of interesting natural features. River Path is perhaps the most popular, and, from its vantage points, you can see the Niagara River Whirlpool and Devil's Hole, the narrowest point of the Niagara River and the scene of an unusual number of tragedies over the years. Footwear suitable for rugged terrain is required.

Location: Niagara Parkway, north of the whirlpool
www.niagaraparks.com/nature/rectrailarea.php

Whirlpool Aero Car

Often called the Spanish Aero Car, because it was designed by Spanish engineer Leonardo Torres-Quevado and built in Spain, the Whirlpool Aero Car is not for the faint of heart—it takes passengers on a half-mile round trip 250 feet above the turbulent waters of the Niagara River, a hair-raising experience for those with a fear of heights. That said, the trip offers an unforgettable bird's-eye view of the Niagara Whirlpool, one that can't be matched from anywhere onshore.

Location: 3850 Niagara River Parkway
www.niagaraparks.com/nfgg/aerocar.php

Notes on Sources

Bailey, George. *Marilyn Monroe and the Making of Niagara.* Niagara Falls, ON: Self-published, 1998.

Berton, Pierre. *Niagara: A History of the Falls.* Toronto, ON: McClelland & Stewart, Inc., 1992.

Cheney, Margaret. *Tesla: Man Out of Time.* New York, NY: Barnes and Noble Books, 1981.

DeVeaux, Samuel. *The Falls of Niagara, or Tourist's Guide to the Wonder of Nature.* Buffalo, NY: William B. Hayden, 1839.

Fraser, Robert L. Fraser. "William Forsyth." *Dictionary of Canadian Biography.* Toronto, ON: University of Toronto Press, 1988.

Gromosiak, Paul. *Water over the Falls: 101 of the Most Memorable Events at Niagara Falls.* Toronto, ON: Royal Specialty Sales, 2006.

Hunt, Inez, and Wanetta W. Draper. *Lightning in his Hand: The Life Story of Nikola Tesla.* Hawthorne, CA: Omni Publications, 1977.

Jasen, Patricia. "Romanticism, Modernity and the Evolution of Tourism on the Niagara Frontier, 1790–1850," *Canadian Historical Review,* 72, September 1991.

Johnson, Paul E. *Sam Patch: The Famous Jumper.* New York, NY: Hill and Wang, 2003.

Kiwanis Club of Stamford, Ontario. *Niagara Falls, Canada: A History of the City and the World Famous Beauty Spot.* Niagara Falls, ON: Kiwanis Club, 1967.

—*Maid of the Mist and Other Famous Niagara News Stories.* Niagara Falls, ON: Kiwanis Club of Stamford, 1971.

Kriner, T.W. *In the Mad Water: Two Centuries of Adventure and Lunacy at Niagara Falls.* Buffalo, NY: J & J Publishing, 1999.

Long, Megan. *Disaster Great Lakes.* Toronto, ON: Lynx Images, 2002.

MacDonald, Cheryl. *Niagara Daredevils.* Canmore, AB: Altitude Publishing, 2003.

Morden, James C. *Historic Niagara Falls.* Niagara Falls, ON: Lundy's Lane Historical Society, 1932.

Parish, Charles Carlin. *Annie Taylor, Queen of the Mist: The Story of Annie Edson Taylor, the First Person Ever to go over Niagara Falls and Survive.* Interlaken, NY: Empire State Books, 1987.

Parson, Horatio. *A Guide to Travelers Visiting The Falls of Niagara*. Buffalo, NY: Oliver G. Steel, 1836.

Peacock, Shane. *The Great Farini: The High-Wire Life of William Hunt*. Toronto, ON: Penguin Books Canada Ltd., 1995.

Petrie, Francis J. *Roll Out the Barrel: The Story of Niagara's Daredevils*. Erin, ON: Boston Mills Press, 1985.

Phillips, David. "The Day Niagara Falls Ran Dry," *Canadian Geographic*, Vol. 109, No. 2, April/May 1989.

Raible, Chris. "Benjamin Lett: Rebel Terrorist," *The Beaver*, October 2002.

Seibel, George A. *Bridges over the Niagara Gorge: Rainbow Bridge 50 years 1941–1991*. Niagara Falls, ON: The City of Niagara Falls, 1990.

—*Ontario's Niagara Parks—100 Years: A History*. Niagara Falls, ON: Niagara Parks Commission, 1985.

Siegel, Scott, and Barbara Siegel. *The Encyclopedia of Hollywood*. New York, NY: Checkmark Books, 2004.

Tiplin, A.H. *Our Romantic Niagara*. Niagara Falls, ON: Niagara Falls Heritage Foundation, 1988.

Vogel, Michael N. *Echoes in the Mist: An Illustrated History of the Niagara Falls Area*. Chatsworth, ON: Windsor Publications Inc., 1991.

Zavitz, Sherman. *Niagara Falls Historical Notes*. St. Catharines, ON: Looking Back Press, 2008.

Other Sources

Interviews with Kevin Harding, Communications Director, Fallsview Casino Resort; George Bailey; Elaine Bald, Theatre Director, IMAX Theatre Niagara Falls; Anne Saks, Director of Marketing, Renaissance Fallsview Hotel; Linda Adair, fifth great granddaughter of William Forsyth.

About the Authors

Andrew Hind and Maria Da Silva are freelance writers who specialize in history and in travel and have a passion for bringing to light little-remembered episodes in history. Together, they have contributed numerous history-related articles to magazine publications. They also conduct guided historical tours, helping people connect with the past in a personal way.

Andrew developed a love for history early on, and he hopes, through his writing, to develop a similar passion to others. Maria has always loved the magic and mystery of Niagara, probably her favorite region, but she never dreamed she would have the opportunity to explore her love of Niagara in the form of a book. *Niagara: Daredevils, Danger and Extraordinary Stories* represents Andrew and Maria's fifth book.